Memorable Characters...
Magnificent Stories

by Susie Garber

SCHOLASTIC
PROFESSIONAL BOOKS

NEW YORK • TORONTO • LONDON • AUCKLAND • SYDNEY
MEXICO CITY • NEW DELHI • HONG KONG • BUENOS AIRES

DEDICATION

To my husband, Bob, and our children,
Elisheva, Rivka, Naftali, Sara Rachel, Avigail and Dina Leah,
and to all those BYQ students who have shared and
continue to share their writing with me.

ACKNOWLEDGMENTS

Special thanks to Wendy Murray for all her magnificent editing and to Joanna Davis- Swing for all her insightful help. Thanks to Rabbi Moshe Neuman, Dean of Bais Yaakov Academy of Queens (BYQ), and to Mrs. Sarah Bergman, the General Studies Principal, who always help me to grow professionally.

And with appreciation for:

- My mentor, Dorothy Marks
- Laurie Pessah, Lucy Calkins and all the wonderful teachers who touched my life at Columbia University Teachers College Reading and Writing Project
- All my colleagues at BYQ who have shared their classrooms with me
- My sister and writing partner, and a great teacher, Mrs. Nancy Schwartz
- My wonderful aunt/editor, Ruth Levine
- My brother-in-law Ken Garber for his insightful professional advice
- My parents for encouraging me to write
- Mrs. Meril Dollman and Mrs. Rose Shulman for taking such good care of my baby so I could write
- All my family and friends for their help and encouragement
- My daughter, Elisheva, for designing the drawings on my reproducibles
- My daughter, Sara Rachel, for contributing her "white spaces" story
- My husband, Bob, for his support and computer help
- I am grateful to God for enabling me to share my book with other teachers

Scholastic Inc. grants teachers permission to reproduce student reproducibles for classroom use only. No other part of this publication may be reproduced in whole or in part, or stored in a retrieval system, or transmitted in any form by any means, electronic, mechanical, photocopying, recording, or otherwise, without written permission of the publisher. For information regarding permission, write to Scholastic Inc., 557 Broadway, New York, NY 10012.

Cover design by Jim Sarfati
Cover photograph by Penny Tweedie/Stone
Interior design by Solutions by Design, Inc.
Interior photographs by Susie Garber

ISBN 0-439-28847-9

Copyright © 2002 by Susie Garber. All rights reserved.
Printed in the U.S.A.

CONTENTS

Introduction 5

CHAPTER 1: 7
Organizing Reading and Writing Time Toward Character Study

CHAPTER 2: 21
What Makes a Character Memorable?
Teaching Students the Key Ingredients

    INTRODUCTORY MINI-LESSON: **Observing Human Nature** 22
        GOAL: *To write notebook entries that have thoughtful observations of people*

    MINI-LESSON 1: **Studying *Madeline* Up Close** 26
        GOAL: *To identify ways authors build characters*

    MINI-LESSON 2: **Tagging Characters** 32
        GOAL: *To write notebook entries that give a character a defining trait*

    MINI-LESSON 3: **Developing Round Characters** 40
        GOAL: *To create more fully-drawn characters*

CHAPTER 3: 47
Memorable Characters Engage Us Emotionally
Teaching Students Basic Ways to Create Likable Characters

    MINI-LESSON 4: **Finding Your Voice** 48
        GOAL: *To write notebook entries that have a strong voice*

    MINI-LESSON 5: **Allowing the Reader to Envision** 54
        GOAL: *To explore what the author wants you to infer about character—learning to spot "white spaces"*

CHAPTER 4: 59
Opposites Attract
Teaching Students How to Use Contrasting Characters to Create Dynamic Plots

    MINI-LESSON 6: **Contrast Builds Conflict** 60
        GOAL: *To chart contrast between the protagonist and the antagonist*

MINI-LESSON 7: **Experimenting With Point of View** 67

> **GOAL:** *To analyze why authors use different points of view*

CHAPTER 5: 73

So What Have You Learned, Dorothy?
Teaching Students How to Build Character Growth Into Their Stories

MINI-LESSON 8: **Change and Growth in Characters** 74

> **GOAL:** *To pinpoint places in books and student writing where characters change*

CHAPTER 6: 79

Hint, Hint
Teaching Students Simple Ways to Use Foreshadowing

MINI-LESSON 9: **Sprinkling Hints About the Plot Within a Character's Traits** 80

> **GOAL:** *To learn to use foreshadowing*

CHAPTER 7: 85

Capturing the Characters in Your Life
Teaching Students How to Fully Sketch People They Know in Memoir Writing

MINI-LESSON 10: **Creating Characters in Memoir** 86

> **GOAL:** *To write memoirs with vivid details and feelings*

Introduction

Sharing a happy publishing moment with Esther

"The foundation of all emotional response in the reader is characterization."
—Maren Elwood

When Sir Arthur Conan Doyle grew tired of his character, Sherlock Holmes, he exercised what he believed to be the writer's privilege. He killed Sherlock off. Doyle's readers protested so much he had to revive him. Readers do grow attached to characters.

When I start the school year in September, Mrs. Piggle-Wiggle brightens those beginning days, beckoning my students to enter the world of stories as I read aloud from Betty MacDonald's memorable series. I anticipate the amazing insights of students year after year as they meet Wilbur, Fern, and Charlotte from *Charlotte's Webb* by E.B. White, Wanda, Maddie, and Peggy from *The Hundred Dresses* by Eleanor Estes, and John Midas from *The Chocolate Touch* by Patrick Skene Catling.

The characters in good books find their way into our hearts because the author has captured *us*, people like us, and people quite different from us. In other words, the author has portrayed human nature.

WRITERS' INSIGHT

Says Milan Kundera, author of *The Unbearable Lightness of Being*: "… The characters in my novels are my own unrealized possibilities…. Each one has crossed a border I myself have circumvented… beyond that border begins the secret the novel asks about...." In *How I Became a Writer*, Phyllis Reynolds Naylor writes: "...In each of my stories, I'm working out for myself and possibly the reader, how I would react in a similar situation...."

Writer Lajos Egri got it right when he said, "character creates plot, not vice versa." When I read a great book, I am pulled into the story by the characters, much the way I am riveted on a bus by a conversation between two people revealing some story of their lives. I may remember a slice of conversation or a facial expression long after the bus ride. When the book ends it is the characters that I remember. I reread my favorite books to revisit these souls. Elizabeth and Mr. Darcy from Jane Austen's *Pride and Prejudice* intrigue me. Anne in *Anne of Green Gables* by L. M. Montgomery is like an old friend, while Irene and Soames from *The Forsyhe Saga* by John Galsworthy draw me into their world.

My students, of course, are no different. They fall in love with characters just as swiftly and permanently as I do. This is something I've known most of my career, teaching students in grades 3 to 6, but it was only recently that I realized I could help my students become better writers by having them use their insights and affinities for book characters to develop characters in their own stories. If published writers use character to drive their stories, why shouldn't my students? And so I began to develop the mini-lessons in this book, which emphasize characterization. I soon discovered that my students wrote stories with more ease. They didn't hit dead ends in their story lines or ramble on aimlessly for pages.

Once students establish a character's personality—a person's quirks, fears, strengths, flaws—then the story's problems and conflicts naturally follow. Student writers are open to many possibilities when they create their own characters. The clear structure helps reluctant writers to open their imagination, too. Some of the student samples included in this book were written by reluctant writers who were transformed into enthusiastic writers. The focus on characterization and prewriting, using the reproducibles in this book, increased the comfort level for these student authors.

I have arranged the book as a series of mini-lessons so you can hear the language I use and the voices of my students, but of course you will make the lessons your own. Many of my students' writings are included so you will know what's possible.

I hope in this book you will find inspiration and ideas to guide you in your important, wonderful work of living and learning with children.

CHAPTER 1

Organizing Reading and Writing Time Toward Character Study

"It is my strongly held belief that reading and writing in schools should have the same reality as reading and writing out of school. If it isn't real, we are wasting our students' time and stunting their language development."

—Mem Fox

A third-grade student author reads her published work.

To set the mini-lessons on character in a context, in this chapter I'll share an overview of my language arts program.

Imagine a classroom where students enthusiastically write and talk about books, a place where creativity crackles in the air. Mine does, thanks to the wonderful teachers at The Reading and Writing Project, Teacher's College, Columbia University, whose philosophies and ideas have helped me to refine my language arts program. Lucy Calkins, Laurie Pessah, Joanne Hindley, Randy Bomer, Ralph Fletcher, Georgia Heard, and Ellin Keene have, if you'll excuse the cliché, taken my breath away with their insights about children's capabilities as readers and writers. These educators and writers and all their forefathers—people like Donald Graves and Donald Murray—have helped me to see the power of helping students to write with the same tools and habits as professional writers. As Lucy Calkins states in *Living Between the Lines:* "the writing classroom is like an art studio where the students' mentors are published authors." I love this metaphor of apprentices to good literature. As a reading and writing educator, I think of the authors of good books as my mentors as well.

A WRITER'S INSIGHT

"I have come to believe that literature provides the best models of language. Through reading, thinking about, discussing, and interpreting great literature, students come to learn most of what they need to know about language— especially if the teacher takes the time to note the demonstrations the literature provides."

—Regie Routman

Writing Time

Writing time includes three phases: a mini-lesson, writing and conferring time, and response and sharing time (Calkins, 1994). The mini-lesson is a short demonstration—5 to 15 minutes—in which the teacher models a skill such as using sensory images or a strategy such as prewriting. Quiet writing and conferring time comprise the heart of the writing time. Response and sharing time usually take place the last 5 to 10 minutes of writing time. The teacher selects a few children to share with the group, or she may have children share their writing with a partner. First she models how students should respond to a fellow author's work. She states the rules and explains that no negative comments are allowed: Students should look for what they like in the piece and then any suggestions, comments or questions must be offered in a constructive tone. The teacher can elicit from children how this can be done and demonstrate the wrong way to respond to a classmate's work.

The Mini-Lesson

What topics do you cover in a mini-lesson? Often you'll take your cues from your students' needs, but in the beginning of the year, develop a list of skills and strategies you know you'll want to address (see lists of ideas, page 12). In September, your mini-lessons will include basic concepts, such as where ideas come from, or how to keep a writer's notebook. To give you a sense of the swift pace and brevity of a mini-lesson, here is how I introduce a writer's notebook:

Holding up my own well-lived notebook, I point out how I jot down possible ideas for stories, colorful words that I've heard or read somewhere and want to remember, and photographs and articles I've clipped to its pages. I tell students that a writer's notebook is a place where a writer records whatever he or she thinks might inspire future writing. Then I ask: What else might you put in your notebook? What would help you write? Together, within a few minutes, we come up with a list like this:

What Goes Into a Writer's Notebook

ideas	dialogue
questions	wish lists
thoughts	I wonders
imaginings	something funny
memories	comic strips
feelings	ideas for stories
poetry	similes
stories	metaphors
pictures	dreams
souvenirs	important things
people you admire	favorite phrases or quotes
personification	

After brainstorming a list such as this, I read a few sample entries by other students about their notebooks, writing, and other subjects. This inspires student authors to write their own wonderful pieces. Take a look at some of my favorites, below, and then try it in your classroom. You'll be amazed at the wonderful insights about writing your students will express.

Notebook

I take out the key
and follow the path
to a small floral door.
It's just my size
right for me
with my favorites, stuck all over it.
I open it up
and what I find
is a world that's just like me
with all the shapes and colors
all which explains my personality.
I let my thoughts flow
to this little room of mine
and when I'm finished for the day
I close my notebook and that's
                    just fine.

—by Chana T., grade 6

9

My Writer's Notebook

My writer's notebook
Is a world all my own.
Each letter is a jewel
Each entry is a crown.
When I open my writer's notebook
I take out each crown
And one by one place each on my head.
When I close my writer's notebook again,
I have a new litter of crowns
Just waiting to be worn.
          —by Michal, grade 6

My Notebook

My notebook is special.
It has a hard cover like a turtle's shell or a rock.
I love writing in my notebook. When I open it there is a rainbow going from
    the beginning to the end
And my stories are the gold from the pot of gold at the end of the
rainbow. I'll never let go of my notebook!!
          —by Esther D., grade 5

Pick Your Notebook

Spiral bound? Blank journal? Looseleaf pages with pockets? Use whatever suits your needs. I've found that students in grades 3 to 6 do well with a bound notebook, so work is not easily torn out or lost. In younger grades I recommend a regular composition notebook which students decorate to make it personalized and special. In grades 5 to 6, students enjoy choosing their own special type of notebook, but I recommend they use one that is bound and not a spiral or looseleaf because work will be lost or torn out.

Shaindy, a third-grade student, shares her writing with a sixth-grade student.

Quiet Writing/Conferring Time

I start out with 10 minutes of quiet writing time, and slowly increase the time so that by October, it's up to 25 minutes. Children become deeply involved in writing because they have chosen what they want to write. During quiet writing time, I confer with students individually to point out strengths in their writing. At the same time I focus on one or two things the writer is ready to try or to improve their use of. (For example, I might ask a child to add more sensory imagery, more feelings, clarify the point of view, and so on. See chart on page 18 for more writing strategies.) Asking a child to attend to more than a couple of matters of craft overwhelms; you want the child to leave a conference with a skip in her step, motivated to work on the piece because she feels informed, guided to see what to address. Lucy Calkins suggests ending a conference with a question such as: "What will you do next?" This engages the writer and invites her to articulate her next step, and motivates her to keep writing.

Response and Sharing Time

During this time, my students read aloud their drafts and published books. No, published doesn't mean they've landed a counter display at Barnes & Noble, but it does mean they have chosen a piece to take all the way through the writing process: revising, editing, proofreading, illustrating, and publishing. Our finished books include a title page, a beautifully designed cover, and a real library card, adhered to endpaper. A child's published work becomes part of our class library. Generally my students publish five to six books a year, though some students publish many more.

One of the joys of teaching is the sparkle in a student's eyes when she proudly displays her own published book. But this doesn't happen overnight. Children must feel confident and accepted as writers before they can share their creativity in class. Each mini-lesson, conference, and a hundred other moments nourish the book—and the writer's confidence—along.

Independent reading time in third grade

Mini-Lessons for the First Three to Four Weeks of School

What goes into a writer's notebook

Looking for ideas

Writing different types of notebook entries (feelings, descriptive entries, lists, memories, imaginings, wonderings, etc.)

Using sensory imagery in writing

Grammar Lessons

How to create an editor's checklist

Capitals

End punctuation

Quotation marks

Paragraphing

Avoiding run-ons

Using correct pronouns

Glittering adjectives (using Ruth Heller's *Luscious Lollipops*)

Vivid verbs (using William Steig's *Brave Irene*)

Mini-Lessons for October Through January

Launching first genre study (picture books)

Noticing characteristics of picture books (repetition, how illustrations and text interact, etc.)

Structure of picture books (circular, snapshot, etc.)

Strong leads

Vivid verbs (substituting verbs for adjectives)

Adding details

Endings

Putting feelings into writing

Introductory character mini-lesson

Focusing a piece

Middle-of-Year Mini-Lessons

Revising and polishing writing (taking out extra words, using stronger verbs)

Writing with voice

Using foreshadowing

White spaces (leaving things to a reader's imagination)

Main ideas and details

Launching more genre studies (memoir, fiction, nonfiction, and poetry)

End-of-Year Mini-Lessons

Letter-writing format (writing to a favorite author describing techniques you appreciate)

Writing more notebook entries with depth and rich language

Combining genres (creating a memoir picture book or a nonfiction poem, etc.)

Revisiting favorite read-alouds and picture books to see what new angles you notice in the author's craft: Does she use short or long sentences? Does she tend to leave a lot of white spaces in her writing? Does she handle transitions in a different way?

Noticing a writer's characteristics in her books (common settings, themes or types of characters, use of descriptive language, etc.)

Eleven Effective Conference Topics

I. Create a list of territories for topics (Atwell, 1988)

2. What more can you add to that entry?

3. Using editor's checklist to self-correct first draft

4. Choosing a notebook entry to develop

5. Help with layout for the final draft (where text and pictures go)

6. Adding more sensory imagery

7. Checking for run-on sentences

8. Use of time and transitions

9. Choosing character names

10. Strong leads

11. Satisfying "ahh" endings

Reading Time

During reading time, each child chooses books to read on her level. When I confer with children during reading time, I teach skills and strategies based on individual needs. I ask my students to keep a separate reading notebook for literary response.

The Mini-Lesson/Focused Read-Aloud

I start reading time with a mini-lesson that focuses on one idea. This could be a reading strategy such as stopping often to recall what you read, summarizing, making inferences, questioning or predicting. Or I might think aloud how I appreciate a literary element such as noticing setting, character or theme (see list below and next page of strategies and literary concepts). Once students are familiar with a literary concept, I may ask them to listen for examples of it as I read aloud. As I read one or two chapters from the shared novel, children follow along in their own copies and use sticky notes to mark places in the text where they see the concept at work. Then students share what they flagged with the class.

Some Reading-Strategy Mini-Lessons

◎ Making personal connections to read-aloud and independent book

◎ Asking questions as you read or listen to read-aloud

◎ Finding parts you can imagine (beautiful language)

◎ Looking for sensory imagery in the text

◎ Looking for new words (discovering ways to figure out words in context)

◎ Making text-to-text connections

◎ Making text-to-world connections

◎ Noticing character traits

Some Literary-Element Mini-Lessons

◎ Finding examples of setting (time and place) in text

◎ Characters (noticing character tags—main trait, flaw or problem)

◎ How time works in the text (noticing flashbacks, pace)

◎ How author shows time passing

◎ Summarizing main story events in a chapter

◎ Summarizing main events in a book

Quiet Reading/Conferring Time

After this discussion, which my students and I call a literary conversation, students read their independent books during quiet reading time, looking for these same concepts. Just as I confer with individual students during quiet writing time, I also confer during quiet reading time. Read-alouds and whole-class literary conversations continue all year. Also, the children write about their books in their reading-response notebooks during this time (see list, below). Talking about and writing about books teaches children to think about what they are reading. As Randy Bomer says in his book *Time for Meaning*, "Literature invites response."

Some Reading-Response Log Assignments

◎ List three new vocabulary words and their definitions. Include the sentences from the book.

◎ Summarize three main events in the chapter.

◎ Write about a question you had while reading.

◎ Write about a part you can really imagine. Cite examples from the text.

◎ Write about a personal connection. What in the text reminded you of something in your life?

◎ Draw a scene or character.

◎ Select a line from the book and write about what it makes you think of or what it reminds you of in your life. How does it connect to what you know about the world or to another book you've read?

Paired Discussion

By mid-October, the children will also read in pairs and have literary conversations with their partners. This usually occurs two times a week, for about 20 minutes. The conversation skills they learn in the whole-class literary discussions guide their paired conversations.

When I listen in on these partner discussions, and as I guide the whole-class literary conversations, I work hard to make sure everyone feels validated when they share ideas.

Especially in the beginning of the year, children need to feel accepted and that they have a voice and an opinion worth noting. As the year progresses, I push children to engage in higher-level interpretative thinking. I ask students to think of discussion questions that will generate different opinions. I encourage them to look for symbolism, to compare different texts, and to search for themes and lessons in a story. I also ask them to think like authors and to try to imagine the author's preliminary work on a book as well as analyzing the author's craft. The concepts and strategies I teach in reading and writing time naturally flow into one another. Literary response and conversation form a bridge between reading and writing time. But, to stretch this metaphor a little more if I may, this current flows because it is properly banked by structures.

To learn about the structures that support a reading and writing classroom, read the must-have classics, such as *Mosaic of Thought* by Ellin Keene, *The Art of Teaching Reading* by Lucy Calkins, *Invitations* by Regie Routman, *Time for Meaning* by Randy Bomer, *When Writers Read* by Jane Hansen, and *Grand Conversations* by Ralph Peterson and Maryann Eeds.

Use the reproducibles on the following pages to help you manage your program. Here is what you will find:

Book Conversation Evaluation sheet (page 17) Use this sheet for assessing individual readers during conferences, partner talks, or small-group book talks. This gives you a general idea of areas your student covers in book conversations.

Use of Reading Strategies (page 18) This list provides the strategies students need to use independently. These skills sheets will help you keep individualized records of your students in both reading and writing.

Writing Conference Record (page 19) Use the sheet to assess individual writers during conferences.

Writing Skills Assessment Checklist (page 20) This is a quick assessment checklist to complete on each student. It will help you gauge areas of strength and areas that need work.

I like to keep a folder for each student with copies of these assessment sheets; as you work with your students, you will adapt them to suit your needs.

Expect the Best—and Wait for Students to Bloom

I expect beautiful writing and I assume and expect my students will grow into avid readers. If a teacher believes in herself and in her students, the children sense this. They will sprout at their own time like the many lovely flowers in a garden.

I recall a new third-grade student, Jenny, who copied into her writing notebook from a dusty basal reader she'd found lying on a back shelf. No matter how I tried to explain to her that she should write her own thoughts, she continued to copy day after day. I grew discouraged and perplexed. I continued with mini-lessons, and smiling encouragement, while I wondered what I should do. Then one day like a burst of sunshine, she sat down without a basal reader on her desk. She opened her notebook and began to write. I watched from across the room, curious. After a while, she approached me timidly. She handed me her notebook. There, scribbled across two pages, sparkled a wonderful story about a time she climbed aboard the wrong bus and ended up in the wrong day camp. Jenny had written a strong beginning, middle, and end. We hugged. From this student I learned the value of waiting, and of having faith that each child unfurls her talent and ability at her own pace. As you develop this type of language arts program and adapt the mini-lessons in this book, I know you will experience similar breakthrough moments with your students.

Student name: _____ Date:_____

Book Conversation Evaluation

The Student Notices:	Comments
Characters' or authors' expression of feelings	
Surprises	
Sequence of main events	
Descriptions of character	
Descriptions of setting	
Funny parts	
Scary parts	
Flashbacks	
Vocabulary that strikes them	
Metaphors and similes	
Personification	
Tone	
Leads and endings	
Illustrations	
Irony	
Personal connections to text	

Use of Reading Strategies

	Good	Okay	Comments
1. Chooses books effectively (has an accurate sense of his/her reading level and is able to find books of high interest to him/her)			
2. Figures out meaning of unfamiliar words (word attacks) using context, dictionary skills			
3. Imagines the story (visualizes)			
4. Identifies with a character			
5. Links the story to personal experience			
6. Questions while reading to make meaning			
7. Makes predictions			
8. Makes inferences (about characters, author's intent, plot, etc.)			
9. Retells, using character names, sequencing, and summarizing skills			
10. In discussions and in writing about the book, identifies main ideas and details			
11. Relates one story to another story			
12. Relates a story to an issue or theme in the world			
13. Skims to find sections to reread for improved understanding			
14. Consistently reads for sustained periods of time in school and at home			

Memorable Characters...Magnificent Stories Scholastic Professional Books

Student name: _____ Conference Date: _____

Writing Conference Record

Title of piece: _____

Main strategies to work on: _____

_____

Student's Strengths	Grammar Skills Exhibited
	Grammar Skills to Work On

Writing Skills Assessment Checklist

1. Effective choice of topic . . . . □

2. Writes with sustained interest . . . . □

3. Revises . . . . □

4. Integrates mini-lesson ideas into writing . . . . □

5. Exhibits good grammar and spelling skills . . . . □

6. Publishes frequently . . . . □

7. Crafts strong leads and endings. . . . . □

8. Writes strong descriptions of setting and characterization . . . . □

9. Organizes thoughts and handles time in writing . . . . □

10. Writes in various genres including nonfiction, interviews, letter writing . . . . . □

12. Uses metaphors and similes . . . . □

13. Integrates concepts such as:

   foreshadowing. . . . . □

   flashback . . . . □

   vivid verbs . . . . □

   sparkling adjectives . . . . □

   details . . . . □

   focusing a piece . . . . □

   identifying and developing important ideas . . . . □

14. proofreads and polishes for publication . . . . □

Memorable Characters...Magnificent Stories Scholastic Professional Books

CHAPTER 2

What Makes a Character Memorable?

Teaching Students the Key Ingredients

Third-grade writers thinking through their ideas.

THE MINI-LESSONS	THE GOALS
Introductory Mini-Lesson: Observing Human Nature	To write notebook entries that have thoughtful observations of people
Mini-Lesson 1: Studying *Madeline* Up Close	To identify ways authors build characters
Mini-Lesson 2: Tagging Characters	To write notebook entries that give a character a defining trait
Mini-Lesson 3: Developing Round Characters	To create more fully-drawn characters

For each mini-lesson, I list several picture books and in some cases, chapter books, so you will have lots of options from which to choose. I find discussing familiar picture book characters effective both in younger and older grades because the characterization techniques can be easily identified in a picture book.

You'll want to read aloud an entire text and have the other texts available for children to look at during writing time. Or you can read part of several texts to illustrate points in your mini-lessons. How much time you spend on the mini-lessons will depend on you taking the pulse of your class. Ideally, a mini-lesson should not exceed 20 minutes and can be as brief as five minutes.

INTRODUCTORY MINI-LESSON

Observing Human Nature

GOAL: *To write notebook entries that have thoughtful observations of people*

"No one can create a character from pure observation: If it is to have life it must be at least in some degree a representation of himself."

—Somerset Maugham

In *Characters Make Your Story*, Maren Elwood says: "Only as the artist or writer understands his fellow man and to that end, sympathizes with him, can he create characters that are lifelike." To achieve this necessary sympathy, writers observe others, and try to understand what makes them tick. This is where writers express their compassion, their empathy, their insight into humankind—whatever the term, the process begins with observation.

With this in mind, I launch my fifth-grade class's study of character by inviting children to observe people they know, and record their observations in notebooks. First, I read aloud something I've written:

People
Some people are like houses with bars on the windows.
Iron gates surround them, all closed in and shut up.
Some people overflow like generous red flowers draping my neighbor's lawn.
They're spontaneous like a squiggly shaped tree.
Sometimes I feel like those houses, all closed in and shut up.
Sometimes I feel flamboyant, like those loud red flowers that beckon fun.
—by Mrs. Garber

After I read my entry aloud I say:

> I wrote this piece while bicycling around the block. I find writing ideas often pop into my head when I am bicycling. Something about the quiet houses I passed—each with a distinct personality, inspired me to write this entry. What do you notice?

Estie: I like how you describe different kinds of people.

Rena: It has feelings too.

Mrs. G.: Where are the feelings? Can you read the lines?

Rena: The part at the end. 'Sometimes I feel like those houses all closed in and shut up. Sometimes I feel flamboyant, like those loud red flowers that beckon fun.'

Leah: I can imagine the red flamboyant squiggly flowers.

Mrs. G.: Think about people you know, and think about yourself. See if you can think about their natures. For example, I can think of people who seem to have a happy nature. When I'm around them I feel cheered. Others make me feel shy, or tense, or sad. Think about people in your family, people in your neighborhood. It could be someone who works in the grocery store or who you see just once, sitting in the park. Then jot down some thoughts or observations about them.

Suggested Books

- *The Art Lesson* by Tomie dePaola
- *Baby* by Patricia MacLachlan
- *Brave Irene* by William Steig
- *Carl's Afternoon in the Park* by Alexandra Day
- ⭐ *Charlotte's Web* by E. B. White
- "Eleven" by Sandra Cisneros, from *Woman Hollering Creek and Other Stories*
- *A Gathering of Days* by Joan W. Blos
- *Harriet's Recital* by Nancy Carlson
- *Imogene's Antlers* by David Small
- ⭐ *The Jolly Postman* by Janet and Allan Ahlberg
- *Loudmouth George & the Sixth-Grade Bully* by Nancy Carlson
- *Madeline* by Ludwig Bemelmans
- *The Magic School Bus* series by Joanna Cole
- *Mirandy and Brother Wind* by Patricia C. McKissack
- *My Rotten, Redheaded Older Brother* by Patricia Polacco
- *The Story of Ferdinand* by Munro Leaf

After writing time, a few students share their notebook entries:

People

People
People are different than each other
Different
Hair
Colors
Styles
People are different than each other

Some are
Fat
Skinny
Tall
Short
People are different

—by Temira, grade 6

Mrs. G.: I like the way Temira points out the physical differences and hints at the deeper differences by repeating, "people are different".

Next Adina shares her piece:

A Heart

A heart has lots of things hidden inside. Some people tell them. Some just hide. It is easier to tell them to get them off of your shoulders. But if you don't, the thoughts get bolder. It keeps special secrets with lots of feelings inside. Everyone has a heart inside of them.

—by Adina, grade 5

Mrs. G.: I like how Adina captured that everyone has something the same inside of them.

Next Reva reads aloud:

Laughter

Laughter is like a big bubble.
Once the bubble is full,
The bubble pops.
Laughter then spills out
from the exploding bubble.
When the streams of laughter fill the air,
it is contagious.
And more bubbles pop.
More laughter streams out
from the bursting bubble.
Everyone has a bubble in them.
You just have to find it.

—by Reva, grade 6

Mrs. G.: I love that Reva says everyone has laughter inside of them, and you just have to find it. What does that say about human nature?

Miriam: I think everyone has happiness but they may not know it.

Finally Shani shares her entry:

What I Need

I don't need jewelry
I don't need a magnet
I don't need money
I don't need a pretty room
I don't need headphones
I don't need a knapsack
All I need is someone warm who loves me.
—by Shani, grade 5

Mrs. G.: Shani expressed a beautiful human value. How would you describe her character, based on this description?

Reva: She loves her family. She doesn't need things that cost money to feel loved.

Mrs. G.: Yes.

Estie: She's kind. She is warm.

Miriam: She loves people.

Mrs. G.: Yes. You see how Shani has begun to create a portrait of her character by revealing her feelings? As we continue to explore characters in books and in our own writing, we will discover many ways a character's nature gets revealed with words.

But for now, as you write, you may wish to just focus on what's inside your heart, as Shani did. And as you write stories about fictional characters, you may want to create a character that is like the one you describe in your entry.

I find this first lesson sets the tone for our character study. Children are eager to explore their budding ideas about human nature, and focusing them on characterization taps into that interest.

Studying *Madeline* Up Close

GOAL: *To identify ways authors build characters*

" . . . I suspect it is when you can write most entirely out of yourself, inside the skin, heart, mind, and soul of a person who is not yourself that a character becomes in his own right another human being on the page."

—Eudora Welty

In a recipe for chocolate chip cookies, you simply mix the proper ingredients in the proper proportions, and if you are good at following directions, the recipe will produce delicious cookies. In creating character, both in literature and in life, there is no such infallible recipe to follow. A pinch of shyness and a smidgeon of humor with four cups of kindness produce all *kinds* of characters!

There's no single way to create a great character, and so, as you will see in the mini-lesson that follows, having the class identify ways in which several authors go about it works well. We write down what we notice on chart paper, and this gives the students a menu of options from which to choose.

I emphasize to students that choosing traits for their characters will help them figure out the plot of their stories, that the character's personality—how she reacts to things, how she views the world—helps to create the problems and hurdles in the narrative. In other words, this character work is time well-spent.

I also read aloud insights and techniques from literature's giants. Students soak up this wisdom like sponges, and appreciate that you share it with them. For example, I tell my students that Ivan Turgenov would grow to know his characters through writing a brief biography of them. Somerset Maugham believed that "He [an author] must understand them [characters] so well, that he will not have to stop and reason out how they will react to any given circumstance or situation."

Maren Elwood breaks the process into three steps:

1. Creating a clear mental concept of the character
2. Selecting one major and two or three minor character traits
3. Presenting these character traits effectively

In this first mini-lesson, I read aloud a familiar picture book, so kids have a head start— they already understand the character. The questions I pose for students are: Exactly how does the author reveal his main character's personality? How does this personality—these character traits—help to build the plot? I know this sounds awfully sophisticated, but with picture books, these questions are relatively easy for kids to answer. For example, in H. A. Rey's *Curious George* books, loveable George's trait of curiosity plunges him into trouble. His curiosity creates the story events.

Here's how I would teach a lesson after reading aloud *Madeline* by Ludwig Bemelmans. Throughout, I'm recording students' ideas on a big sheet of chart paper.

Mrs. G.: What is Madeline like? How would you describe her personality?

Illana: She's brave.

Mrs. G.: How do you know that?

Adina: She walks on the edge of the bridge. Look at the picture.

Mrs. G.: Great. I hadn't thought of that illustration at all. Actually, that shows it's a true picture book because we are getting some of the information from the text and some from the illustrations. Walking on the edge of the bridge shows she is daring and brave. She's the only one doing this. What else tells you she is brave or different?

Adina: She says, "Pooh, pooh," to the tiger.

Mrs. G.: Yes. And that is a great example of how an author uses a character's speech to show her personality. She stands up to something scary. It shows she has courage and spirit. Can you find another example of the character's personality?

Leah: The author says: "She was not afraid of mice and she loved winter snow and ice."

Mrs. G.: Good. So how do we find out about Madeline in that example?

Leah: The author tells us about her.

Mrs. G.: Good. So far we discovered that character is built by what the character says or does or information the author tells about the character.

Dani: The author also says that she was the smallest. So she's different. And that "Nobody knew so well, how to frighten Miss Clavel."

Leora: She has a good imagination. She sees the crack on the ceiling as a rabbit.

Mrs. G.: So how did the author let us know that?

Leora: The author tells us, and it's also like he tells Madeline's thoughts.

Adina: Madeline likes to be different. She didn't walk in line.

Naomi: I agree. Madeline is different. She is the only one not crying.

Mrs. G.: So we can tell what she is like through her actions, too.

After this conversation, we review the notes on our chart and then compile a new list that synthesizes our ideas:

Ways Authors Reveal Characters

◎ The author tells us information about the character
   ("She loved winter snow and ice.")

◎ The character talks
   (She said, "Pooh, pooh," to the tiger.)

◎ Author uses illustrations
   (She's walking on the edge of the bridge.)

◎ What the character does
   (She's going up to the mice. She imagines the crack on the ceiling being a rabbit.)

◎ What other characters say about the character

◎ The character's thoughts and feelings

To wrap up the mini-lesson, I point out that in shorter books, such as *Madeline* and other picture books, the author usually creates his character by emphasizing one trait. (Even in longer books, one trait often dominates.) The students agree that in Madeline's case, the author portrays her as brave or daring.

Post a chart like the one at the right in your classroom. Students can refer to it while listening to a read-aloud or when reading their independent books. You could also hand it out for students to fill in.

How Authors Reveal Characters

Title _____

Author _____

Character _____

What character says

Thoughts

Actions

Feelings

How character responds
to other characters

What author tells
about the character

Chart created by a sixth-grade class

"Avoid depicting the hero's state of mind; you ought to try to make it clear from the hero's actions."

—Anton Chekhov

Students Pair Up to Look for Characterization in Picture Books

After this lesson I ask students to work in pairs for about 20 minutes to analyze several picture books. I ask them to look for examples of how authors reveal character and to write on sticky notes what they find, using the chart to remind them of the techniques to be on the look out for.

Next, we regroup as a class for ten minutes and the students share what they found.

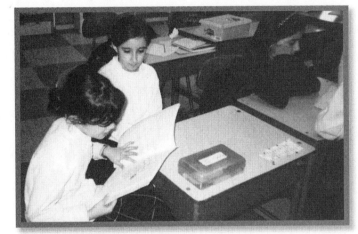

A third grader shares her watercolor painting of two characters.

BUILDING ON THE MINI-LESSON:

Depicting Character Through Illustration

In a follow-up mini-lesson, the students and I look at how a picture-book character's personality is further conveyed by the illustrations. As we saw with *Madeline,* the illustrations and text work together in a picture book. Before I read aloud *Imogene's Antlers,* written and illustrated by David Small, I ask students to notice the details of Imogene's personality in the illustrations.

To get students started, I point out how in one picture of Imogene going to bed, her toys and her shoes remain on the bed, suggesting that Imogene is disorganized and perhaps dreamy. She doesn't focus so much on her immediate surroundings. Pointing to another picture, in which Imogene awakens with antlers, I venture that David Small wants us to perceive Imogene as imaginative. The pictures of the mother fainting and her horrified expressions characterize the mother as proper and unable to understand her daughter. After I share my interpretations of a few illustrations, I invite students to try this on their own, as we look at other pictures in the book. Students delight in examining the illustrations for details of personality. This activity can be done as a whole-class lesson, or in small groups or pairs.

Personality-Rich Picture Books

In *The Magic School Bus* series by Joanna Cole, Miss Frizzle's outfit, jewelry, and shoes conform in meticulous detail to the scientific subject matter being taught. We discuss how illustration reinforces the character's traits. Miss Frizzle's imaginative, outlandish outfits reflect her unusual teaching style and personality.

In *Carl's Afternoon in the Park* by Alexandra Day, an entire story is told through illustration. I ask students to describe the baby's personality. The baby is depicted in the illustrations as adventurous and capable of taking care of herself. Then they describe the dog Carl as fun-loving and attentive to the baby. In one picture he gives her a balloon. The students notice that Carl watches the baby in every illustration, and the baby points to where the baby wants to go. One student notices the baby is generous; to support her point she refers to an illustration in which the baby shares her ice cream cone with Carl.

Students Illustrate a Character

Once students have studied how authors use illustrations to convey character (this usually takes two or three days), I ask them to dream up a character, and try to depict his or her personality traits through their own illustrations. I ask them to include details such as hairstyle, jewelry, type of clothing, facial expression, characteristic objects, what the character is doing or saying, setting, and even a person's thoughts in a bubble. For

many children drawing is a smooth entry point into writing. Through the details in their art, students can develop character, story line, and ideas. In this next example, watch how a character-based drawing and a brief conversation with me allowed this student to open up and write a distinctive poem.

> **Mrs. G.:** This is a lovely drawing. I am just curious. Why isn't the sun smiling?
>
> **Sharon:** Because he was tired.

This answer intrigued me.

> **Mrs. G.:** What do you mean?
>
> **Sharon:** The sun is tired because he has to stay up so long. You know, how the night doesn't come until like seven or eight.
>
> **Mrs. G.:** Sharon, that's so interesting. I hadn't thought about the sun getting tired. I think you just wrote a poem or a story.

Sharon looked surprised.

Mrs. G.: It's so good. Please go write it down. I can't wait to read it.

Here is what Sharon wrote:

> ### Sun
> It's not smiling because it's tired.
> The sun sometimes is tired
> because when it goes up, it hardly has sleep.
> It only has a few hours at night.
> It stays up the whole day so
> late until seven or eight.
> —by Sharon, grade 3

Drawing often opens up student writers' imaginations to all sorts of possibilities in creating characters.

Tagging Characters

GOAL: *To write notebook entries that give a character a defining trait*

" . . . Certain characteristics have to be selected, characteristics that logically go together. Even these cannot be given equal importance. Almost always one is emphasized above all others. This is because the human mind is forever demanding unity, cohesion, pattern, in everything it sees."

—Maren Elwood

Now that students have written notebook entries about human nature, analyzed the ways authors reveal character, and created a character-based illustration, they are ready to learn how to give their character a tag. Tagging a character means to give a specific, fine-tuned detail to a character (Conrad, 1990). Here's how I begin the mini-lesson:

Part One: *Discuss Various Books*

Mrs. G.: Today we are going to explore how the characters in the books we read each have one outstanding trait that makes us remember them. When I say this character's name, call out what you think of: Pierre.

Leah: He doesn't care.

Mrs. G.: Great. Now think about how Pierre's not caring played out.

Dina: He stayed home when his parents went out. He said he didn't care, even when the lion came to call.

Mrs. G.: Yes. His trait of not caring set the whole story in motion, kind of like a snowball rolling downhill. Pierre's problem—his not caring—created the plot or the story problem. How did the story end?

Renee: Pierre was swallowed by the lion and he learned to care.

Mrs. G.: Yes. He changed and the not caring stopped. This personality trait or flaw led to the story's resolution.

As we continue the lesson, I guide students to understand that the tag is almost one and the same with the story problem. I want students to begin to see that story plot is driven by the tag.

I ask students to think of picture-book characters with particularly outstanding traits.

Together, we discuss these character traits, and I jot down their ideas on chart paper. Some characters that lend themselves to this discussion are as follows. *Note: The story problems in all of these books equal the main character's dominant characteristic trait, or tag.*

- Amelia Bedelia (*Amelia Bedelia* series by Peggy Parrish), who takes what people say literally
- Curious George (*Curious George* series by H. A. Rey), who is always curious
- Pierre (*Pierre* by Maurice Sendak), who only says, "I don't care."
- Harriet (*Harriet's Recital* by Nancy Carlson), who is afraid of dancing in her recital.
- Tomie (*The Art Lesson* by Tomie dePaola), who wants to be an artist but resists the teachers' rules about art.

Part Two: *Look at One Picture Book in Depth*

Now we're ready to look at how author Munro Leaf used a tag for the main character in *The Story of Ferdinand.* Ferdinand, a gentle bull, prefers sitting and smelling flowers under his cork tree to fighting with the other bulls. Alas, when a bee sting causes him to appear fierce, he is chosen to be in a bullfight. His true personality shines as he sits quietly in the bullring and smells the flowers in the ladies' hair. The disappointed bullfighters return him to his cork tree. Clearly, the story problem (that Ferdinand doesn't act like a bull) developed from the character's tag: gentleness.

After reading aloud the story once for our enjoyment, I introduce the lesson.

Mrs. G.: Authors sometimes use a technique called tagging characters. It means giving a character one outstanding trait or detail, which the author reinforces in just about every scene. I am going to read aloud *The Story of Ferdinand* again. Listen for the tag or identifying trait of Ferdinand, and examples of this tag throughout our story.

After my second reading, I had the following conversation with students:

Rina: Ferdinand is quiet. He doesn't like to butt and fight like the other bulls.

Mrs. G.: Good. So Ferdinand's actions show us what he does and does not like to do.

Adina: Ferdinand is calm.

Esther: He's independent. He does his own thing.

Mrs. G.: Where do we see that?

Esther: He goes off by himself to smell the flowers. He doesn't want to fight in the bullfights in Madrid like the other bulls.

Dani: I wouldn't mind having him for my brother. My brothers fight.

Shani: He doesn't care what others think.

Risha: He's quieter.

Rena: He's different. He likes to sit in one spot and smell the flowers.

Leora: Ferdinand reminds me of myself. After homework every night, I lie on my bed and read quietly.

Naomi: He acted that way no matter what happened. He always acts the same.

Mrs. G.: Good. So what is Ferdinand's character tag—his identifying characteristic?

Leora: It says he likes to sit quietly and smell flowers.

Mrs. G.: Can you find examples in the text where he does this?

Rina: In the beginning he smells flowers under the cork tree.

Leah: He does it at the bullfight when he smells the flowers in the ladies' hair.

Mrs. G.: Yes. The author keeps reiterating this action. The author accomplishes this by telling us that Ferdinand likes to smell the flowers and then the author shows us the character doing this action. (I point to our chart on How Authors Reveal Characters.)

Also, notice the illustrations. How is Ferdinand characterized?

Elisheva: He has this tiny head peeking out at the bullfight and his name is printed so tiny.

Mrs. G.: Using *The Story of Ferdinand*, I want to model for you how to fill out a character tag sheet (see reproducible, page 38). This sheet will help you with your writing.
Under "character name" we fill in "Ferdinand the Bull."

There is a space to draw an illustration of him. I would want to draw him in a way that conveys his personality. I might show his big eyes and his gentle expression. Now in the tag space, what word would you use to describe his characteristic trait?

Chevie: He likes to sit and smell the flowers. He's gentle.

Mrs. G.: Okay. Now at the bottom we list three events where the author demonstrated his tag.

Leora: In the beginning he sits quietly and smells the flowers instead of fighting with the other bulls.

Rina: He doesn't want to be chosen to fight in the bullfights. He'd rather sit under his tree and smell the flowers.

Naomi: When he is chosen he just sits in the bullring and quietly smells the flowers in the ladies' hair.

Mrs. G.: Good. Do you notice any connection between the story events and the character's tag?

Rina: The tag is the problem.

Mrs. G.: Yes. Could you say that here the tag—Ferdinand's gentle nature—generates the story events?

Naomi: Yes. Because Ferdinand is not like the other bulls and that's what the story is about.

Mrs. G.: Exactly. So the story line grows from the character.

Part Three: *Introduce the Character Tag Sheet*

The goal of this next phase of the mini-lesson is for students to decide on a main character and its tag, and to sketch story events based on this tag. I hand out a tag sheet (p.38) to students and tell them that it is a prewriting outline. It is important for students to understand the concept of prewriting, so that they can keep control of their stories. I find the reproducible very helpful with both younger and older students, and with struggling writers. Here's how I introduce it:

> **Mrs. G.:** You may use this sheet to help you take notes before you create a story. You may glue the tag sheet into your writer's notebook. Sometimes the tag will help you think of the character's name. Next you can create an illustration of the character. Sketching details may help you imagine the character. Then at the bottom of the sheet list three possible story events that could unfold based on your character's personality. These event or plot ideas will give you a direction. Don't worry if you revise these or add different ones.

Part Four: *Examine Another Picture Book*

(or continue on another day)

To guide students to the next step of developing story events, I read aloud the picture book *Loudmouth George and the Sixth-Grade Bully* by Nancy Carlson, which has a clear story line based on the main character's fear. I point out how the conflict and story problem grew from George's fear of the sixth-grade bully, who kept stealing his lunch. George is afraid to go anywhere, and he can't pay attention in school. How George will solve his problem creates suspense. George's character tag (fear of the bully) equals the story problem. I point out to students how the author presents the problem and then the problem gets worse. The bully keeps demanding more lunch, and George is always hungry. Then the solution comes through George with the help of his friend Harriet. The main character has to solve the story problem. It is George himself who has to earn a reprieve from the bully.

In the student sample on page 36, Chani and Talia, two fifth graders, created a little bunny whose tag was shyness. Listing the story events on the tag sheet helped them structure their story around the tag. I like the way they described the character in detail in the beginning of the story. They eventually went on to publish this piece as a picture book.

Teaching Tip for Younger Students

Please note that with younger students, I don't ask them to list story events the first day. Instead, the next day I teach a follow-up lesson (see below) and then they are ready to list their story events on the tag reproducible. For older students, depending on time, I include the follow-up lesson as part of the first mini-lesson since they will be able to assimilate more concepts at once.

Teaching Tip for Older Students

During the mini-lesson, and as you guide students to use the character tag sheet, enrich students' understanding of characterization by coming at it from different angles, and by using various terms. For example, expand the definition of a trait by discussing a character's flaw, or need, or fear. Ask such questions as: What is your character's flaw? What does he most fear or worry about? What does he want? What does he dream of doing? What does he need?

The Little White Rabbit

This little white rabbit is as soft as a baby's cheek. His blue pair of eyes shimmer like the golden sun. His small little tail shaped like a button is as soft as a little cotton ball. His cute little nose sniffs some carrots that his small red lips love to munch on.

His small pair of feet walks one by one to his home in an entryway. His ears hear his little furry friends from miles away. As the little white rabbit blinks his eyes his eyelashes curl together like a small girl's hair.

His cheeks are as smooth as the soft snow in the cold winter.

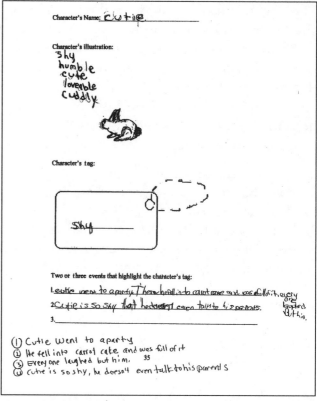

Chani and Talia's Character Tag Sheet

Even when this little rabbit's aunts and uncles come over and say how adorable he is, he is too shy to say, "I know." When he goes to a birthday party and they give out carrot cake, he looks at himself and everybody laughs. He realizes he is covered in cake. He just couldn't laugh with them. He is too shy.

When this little rabbit grows up, he is not shy with his friends. They jump on the bed and swing on the swings. I am happy because he's mine.

—by Chani and Talia

In this next example, it's clear that filling out the character tag sheet helped Esther structure her story.

Jack the Mean Boy

There once was a boy named Jack. He had brown hair and blue eyes. He was eight years old and in second grade. Jack was always making kids cry. He would make faces at them and tell them "get out of my way." That second the hall would be cleared. One day Jack saw a big and heavy rock on the floor. He picked it up and threw it at a window. The next minute he heard an alarm go off. So he ran away. The next morning Jack went to school with his mean and bad attitude, bossing kids around. When the teacher came in the room, Jack was still in the back of the room playing ball. When the teacher told him to go to his seat, he quickly ran to the last seat in the middle row.

As the day went on, Jack got more and more bored. Finally, the bell rang. Jack grabbed his knapsack and went through the hall. He made faces at all the kids until he got home.

At home Jack's mother told him that she heard on the news that a child threw a rock at a window and hit someone on the head but luckily she was okay. After Jack heard what his mother told him, he felt really bad and almost cried. Jack ran to the child's house, and told the police that he threw the rock, and he would pay the price. The officer told Jack that he did the right thing for telling him and that he would have to earn money to replace the window. When Jack got home he decided not to be mean anymore because he could really hurt someone.

—by Esther, grade 5

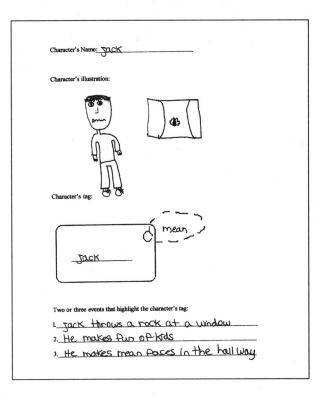

Two pages from Esther's published picture book, "Jack the Mean Boy."

Name: _____ Date: _____

Character Tag Sheet

Character's name: _____

_____

Character's illustration:

_____

Character's tag:

_____

Two or three events that highlight the character's tag:

1. _____

2. _____

3. _____

Memorable Characters...Magnificent Stories   Scholastic Professional Books

Readers'-Response Log on Characters

To link the previous writing mini-lesson to my students' reading, I ask them to write reader-response entries about characters from their independent books or the class-shared novel, focusing on character tags and identifying objects. Analyzing an author's craft helps students with their own writing and literature. Many books on writing stress that writers must read to become writers. I find it opens a whole new world to read like an author; I notice so many craft techniques to try. Student writers also need models to become adept at creating characters.

Third-grade students look for tags in independent reading books

In the following entries, students make observations about characters in *Charlotte's Web* by E. B. White, which we read as a class novel.

Charlotte

Wilbur thinks Charlotte is bossy because she tells Wilbur what to do—like to go to sleep. Most of the animals in the barn don't like her because she is bossy. Also flies don't like her because they get stuck in her webs. She talks differently, like she says, "Salutations."

    —by Etti, grade 3

Fern

Fern is acting very weird. She hears the animals talking. My favorite part is when Wilbur kept asking Charlotte if he could do so many things before bed. I liked it because Charlotte was like his mother and because it was funny.

    —by Adina G., grade 3

Using the Tag Sheet With Picture-Book Characters

I have my students work in pairs to fill out the Character Tag Sheet. I ask them to focus on a character in their independent book or in one of the following picture books: *Contrary Mary* by Anita Jeram, *Imogene's Antlers* by David Small, *Amelia Bedelia,* by Peggy Parrish, *Pierre* by Maurice Sendak, *Curious George* by H. A. Rey, *Copycat* and *Ruby the Copycat* by Peggy Rathmann.

Analyzing character tags, and the story events that highlight them, shows students how to use such tags in their own writing. I ask students to write down any ideas they notice that will help them with their stories.

Developing Round Characters

GOAL: *To create more fully-drawn characters*

> "The test of a round character is whether it is capable of surprising in a convincing way. If it never surprises, it is flat."
>
> —E. M. Forster

Flat characters, which have one main character trait and always act predictably, are a great place for beginning writers to start experimenting with character, but soon they'll want to explore creating more complex characters. Typically, a flat character inhabits a children's short story or a picture book. Round characters are drawn with more traits. Authors develop round characters in longer stories and novels, though they may also include flat characters. We usually refer to these as minor characters.

To launch this mini-lesson, I use one of my favorite books, *Brave Irene* by William Steig. I chose this book because Irene, even though she is a picture-book character, is portrayed with enough intricacy that I consider her a round character. Irene is brave and persevering when she trudges through a blizzard to deliver the gown her mother sewed for the duchess, yet, as you will see in the following book discussion, Steig weaves layers of character into Irene.

Mrs. G.: There are two types of characters—flat and round. A flat character has one or two traits. This type of character is usually found in a picture book. When a character has more traits, we say that the character is a round character. Why do you think we use the terms *flat* and *round*?

Sprintzy: Maybe like three-dimensional is round?

Mrs. G.: Yes, that's it. The character is three-dimensional, fully rounded, life-like. We usually find round characters in longer books. Of course a chapter book can have some flat characters and sometimes in a picture book the author creates a round character. In this book I'm about to read to you, we learn a lot about Irene's personality from what she says, her actions, and what others say about her. We also are told her thoughts. See if you think Irene is a round character or a flat character. Look for examples of her personality traits.

After I read aloud, we have the following discussion:

Shani: Irene cares what her mother says, and she cares about her mother.

Leora: She never gives up. For example, when she has no way to reach the palace from the hill, she decides to make the box into a sled. Also, she begs her mother to let her go. She doesn't give up even after the dress blows away.

Deena: Irene is brave to go in the snow. I can imagine the box and the dress blowing Irene along.

Chedva: Irene has a good imagination. She imagines the wind talking and telling her to go home. She's a determined person. She twisted her ankle but she kept going. I once twisted my ankle, and I didn't go to ballet.

Leora: She imagines how the duchess and her mother would feel.

Miriam: She kissed her mother six times.

Adina: She's smart. At the top of the cliff, she used the box as a sled. She's cheerful. When she's stuck, she doesn't give up. She gets up and keeps trying.

Mrs. G.: Adina, can you show us some examples of this in her thoughts?

Adina: Well, when the gown blows away, she decides to trudge on with just the box.

Mrs. G.: Good. Do you think of her as a round or a flat character?

Miriam: I think she's round because she has a lot of traits and like you can't always predict what she'll do. Like when she almost got buried in snow and was going to give up and then she pulled herself out.

Mrs. G.: Good. It's true that a round character is someone who surprises us. Good point. We glimpse her thoughts when she was almost ready to stay buried in the snow and then it says, "And never see her mother's face again? Her good mother who smelled like fresh-baked bread. In an explosion of fury, she flung her body about to free herself." Let's go ahead and list some of Irene's traits.

Our discussion generates the following chart:

◎ Brave (She went out in the blizzard.) Also, in the last lines of the book, the note says, "What a brave and loving person Irene was. Which, of course, Mrs. Bobbin knew, better than the duchess." Here we see other characters' opinions of her.

◎ Determined and positive (She never gave up, even when the gown blew away and she got buried in snow.)

◎ Smart (She used the box as a sled, and she found the palace.)

◎ Loving (She tucked in her mother with kisses and took the package for her.)

◎ Optimistic. She makes the best of things. (She enjoyed the ball.)

Mrs. G.: Now that we've discussed round characters, let's look at the characters in our class novel. Think about the characters in *Charlotte's Web* and decide whether any seem round or flat. Remember, flat characters always act predictably. Round characters, like real people, can surprise us.

Naomi: Charlotte's very wise.

Mrs. G.: How do you know?

Naomi: I know she's wise because she watches Wilbur, and she decides she likes his character. Also, she's good because she tries to be friends with Wilbur because he's lonely.

Mrs. G.: Would you call her flat or round?

Leora: I think she's round because she surprises the reader when she catches the fly, and we see she's bloodthirsty, but she has lots of other traits like being kind and a good friend and smart and wise.

Mrs. G.: Excellent.

Shani: I think she's round, too. Charlotte cares about herself and others, and she's smart. When Wilbur said, "You're eating insects and it's awful," Charlotte explained insects would overrun the world if she didn't eat them. She surprised me because it seemed cruel when she ate the bug, but then she explained it wasn't.

[The discussion continues.]

Mrs. G.: So we seem to agree that Charlotte is a round character. She has lots of traits. Let's list the traits and some examples.

Dani: Charlotte is like a mother. She likes to be in charge. She tells Wilbur to go to sleep, and she tells him not to worry.

Miriam: She's a good friend. She just met Wilbur, and she's nice to him.

Sara: She's smart. She figures out how to save Wilbur, and she's also independent like Ferdinand the bull. On page 40 it says, "I live by my wits."

Mrs. G.: She's practical. Can you find an example of that?

Leora: She has to catch bugs to survive so she does.

Mrs. G.: Where do we see this?

Leora: On page 40 it says, "You have your meals brought to you in a pail. Nobody feeds me. I have to get my own living. I live by my wits."

Rachel: She's a good writer, because she writes the right words in the web to save Wilbur.

Chedva: She is also humble. She says, "I'm not as flashy as some, but. . ."

I encourage students to support their ideas with text. I ask them to use the chart as reference to categorize what strategy this author uses to convey character and I compliment my students on their astute observations. As they continue reading *Charlotte's Web*, students continue to look for ways E. B. White uses techniques of characterization. Students add to a list, which we keep posted on the wall.

Techniques E.B. White Uses to Create Character in *Charlotte's Web*

1. What the character says and does.

2. What other characters say about her.

3. What the author says about her.

4. The character's thoughts and feelings.

By finding examples of character traits and identifying if a character is round or flat, students learn to think about what they read. The more details they notice in good literature, the more they can transfer these ideas to their own writing.

BUILDING ON THE MINI-LESSON:

Practicing Characterization in Journals, Diaries, or Letters

Now that students have analyzed round characters in a read-aloud and a class novel, they are ready to try out a round character in their writing. I invite them to write a letter, journal, or diary entry because in first-person narration, it's relatively easy to reveal several traits. I suggest that students list a few traits they wish to develop in their entry, and think about ways the character will surprise the reader. I remind them that flat characters always act the same and round characters don't. I show students some books where authors create characters through letters or diary entries. While portraying a round character is a stretch for many students—and adult writers—using literature as a model encourages all the student writers to try.

I read an excerpt from the Newbery book *A Gathering of Days* by Joan W. Blos:

> Providence, Rhode Island
> November 20, 1899
>
> To my namesake, Catherine
>
> I give you this book on your fourteenth birthday, as I turned fourteen the year of the journal: the year that was also my last on the farm tho' I did not know it then. It was also the year that my father remarried, and my best friend, Cassie, died. Cassie lives in my memory still, of all of us the only one never to grow old.
>
> Once I might have wished for that: never to grow old. But now I know that to stay young always is also not to change. And that is what life's all about—changes going on every minute, and you never know when something begins where its going to take you. So one thing I want to say about life is don't be scared and don't hang back, and most of all, don't waste it.
>
> Your loving great-grandmother,
> Catherine Hall Onesti

Mrs. G.: In this example, the character's personality comes through in terms of word choice, ideas, and way of speaking. What traits do you notice?

Chani: She's a thoughtful person. She thinks about life and how it's full of changes.

Mrs. G.: Good. She's a positive thinker. She sees the good in growing old.

Suri: She sees how we can learn from all of life's experiences, even sad ones.

Mrs. G.: Where do you see that?

Suri: When she says her friend died and never grew old. It's very sad, but she learned it's good to grow old because life is full of changes.

Mrs. G.: She is a round character because she exhibits several traits in this diary excerpt. She is a person I'd like to meet and make friends with.

Next, I encourage students to bring in other books where authors characterize through letters or diaries. Someone notices that in *From the Mixed-Up Files of Mrs. Basil E. Frankweiler* by E. L. Konigsburg the whole story is told in a letter and a file to Saxonberg. Mrs. Frankweiler's personality is round, and the author portrays her traits using this letter-writing format:

> To my lawyer, Saxonberg:
>
> I can't say that I enjoyed your last visit. It was obvious that you had too much on your mind to pay any attention to what I was trying to say. Perhaps, if you had some interest in this world besides law, taxes, and your grandchildren, you could almost be a fascinating person. Almost. That last visit was the worst bore. I won't risk another dull visit for a while, so I'm having Sheldon, my chauffeur, deliver this account to your home.

Mrs. G.: What traits do you notice in Mrs. Frankweiler?

Esti: Mrs. Frankweiler is a self-assured person.

Tami: She has no patience for flaws in others.

Dina: She is well-educated and smart. I can tell by how she speaks and the words she chooses.

Mrs. G.: Can you give an example?

Tami: Like in these sentences: "It was obvious that you had too much on your mind to pay any attention to what I was trying to say. Perhaps, if you had some interest in this world besides law, taxes, and your grandchildren…."

Suri: You can tell she's wealthy because she has a chauffeur. And she isn't afraid to tell her feelings. She's very direct. Like when she says, "I can't say I enjoyed your last visit."

Mrs. G.: Good. The author portrays Mrs. Frankweiler's traits as a round character in this letter-writing format.

Next, I ask students to try to create a round character. They can choose to write a letter, or a journal entry, or some other format if they wish. The following is an excerpt from published student work:

Aliza, a fifth grader, shares her published book.

The Diary of Golden Curls Daughter of Bowana

April 15, 1870

Dear Diary,

It's my birthday and even though Father and my friends gave me lots of presents (you are one of them), I'm both mad and sad. Sad because today is the anniversary of Mother's death, and mad because Father told me that since it is my 15th birthday, I must wed. And to EVIL WEEVIL!! That awful man! Father agrees with me, but he says, and I quote, "We must make peace between the two towns, and you're the one to do it. Besides, I'll make him stay here so I can keep an eye on him." Why must I be the one to do all the awful jobs? Oops, I'm getting ahead of myself. You see we live in a part of the world that's forsaken except for us, Bowy and that other dumb town, Dradrad. We are called Bowy because we are good at bows and arrows. I admit we're pretty foolish, but we're clever in our own way. Dradrad is so boring. That's why they call it Dradrad. They have the most modern weapons (for instance, Hotshot Boms, Speed Arrows), but since the mermaids, faeries and wood dwellers, dwarves, and elves (meaning all faery creatures) scorn them, they are not good with weapons because no faery creature will help them, and it's useless for them to try to learn how to use weapons without help from faery creatures. After all that, I ask you Diary to tell me why I have to marry Evil Weevil, the dumb son of that dumb mayor of Dradrad. Good-bye Diary for now. My father's calling me.

why **I** have to marry Evil Weevil, the dumb son of that dumb mayor of Dradrad. Goodbye, Diary, for now. My father's calling me.

April 20, 1870

Dear Diary,

I know I haven't written to you for a few days, but it's not my fault. I'll tell you what happened. Right after I stopped writing, I found out that the wedding was supposed to be on April 21, **TO-MORROW**. I fumed and fretted until now, when I had to pour out my thoughts to you. So here they are! Hold out the bowl! A little bit of humor. I bear my husband abolishes humor. What will I do, with no humor? O Diary, I have tons of questions with no answers. If I was saying that, my voice would have risen alarmingly. Goodbye, Diary.

April 22, 1870

I wanted to write right after the wedding, but I was tired, because Evil Weevil must have pinched me 15 times, one for each year I lived. I hate that man!! I guess I can answer the question about whether that man is as awful as the story goes or not. The answer is **YES**!! Yes 1,000 times over!! He is **SO** awful. He's one of those men who think women can't do fun manly things but only hard, dumb, manly things. **I HATE HIM**. See you later, Diary.

←Evil Weevil, & I late him!!

A page from Aliza's published book.

April 20, 1870

Dear Diary,

I know I haven't written to you for a few days, but it's not my fault. I'll tell you what happened. Right after I stopped writing, I found out that the wedding was supposed to be on April 21. TOMORROW. I fumed and fretted until now, when I had to pour out my thoughts to you. So here they are! Hold out the bowl!

A little bit of humor. I bet my husband abolishes humor. What will I do with no humor? Oh Diary, I have tons of questions with no answers. If I was saying that, my voice would have risen alarmingly. Good-bye Diary.

—by Aliza, grade 5

In Aliza's diary excerpt, the character, Golden Curls, shows she's smart with her good vocabulary and refined in her way of thinking and speaking. She's also very emotional: "If I was saying that, my voice would have risen alarmingly." And she's a good storyteller. She surprises the reader and has many traits, so we say she is a round character.

Identifying Flat and Round Characters
Have students divide into pairs or small groups to identify three characters in their independent books. Make sure they use examples from the text to show why the characters are flat or round. This activity leads to writing short essays on a flat or round character with supporting evidence from the text.

CHAPTER 3

Mindy shares her published book with her peers.

Memorable Characters Engage Us Emotionally

Teaching Students Basic Ways to Create Likable Characters

THE MINI-LESSONS	THE GOALS
Finding Your Voice	To write notebook entries that have a strong voice
Allowing the Reader to Envision	To explore what the author wants you to infer about character—learning to spot "white spaces"

Finding Your Voice

GOAL: *To write notebook entries that have a strong voice*

> "Get so well acquainted with your characters that they live and grow in your imagination exactly as if you saw them in the flesh: and finally tell their story with all the truth and tenderness and severity you are capable of."
>
> —Katherine Anne Porter

One way students can achieve a round character is through voice, and so this is the craft matter we look at next. In a strong piece of writing, whether it's a newspaper account of a factory closing or a nineteenth-century novel, the voice of the narrator shines through. We "hear" the person behind the words, we sense his or her personality. As Ralph Fletcher says in *Live Writing*, the writing sounds honest, authentic. "As a writer you've got to give the narrator a compelling voice," Fletcher advises. Voice has the power to evoke emotions in the reader. Without it, writing is flat, like a dull political speech.

Students sometimes ask me: What's the difference between a character's voice and the author's voice? That's a tough question. They are distinct, and perhaps the better the writer, the more distinct they are, but a character's voice is never one-hundred percent pure, I tell students. In his book, Fletcher addresses this point with a quote from Han Nolan: "…you can still get hints of the author through the [character's] voice…. It's like leaving fingerprints all over a glass. The author's fingerprints are all over the stories."

This is sophisticated stuff, and even published novelists continue to struggle with and learn about voice. With elementary-age students, the baby steps into voice are nonetheless worth taking. The first step in my classroom is to help students see that revealing feelings in their writing often results in strong voice. That way, the reader feels the narrator is a real person.

After conducting the mini-lesson that follows, I ask students to write notebook entries as first-person narrators. Later, they will use voice to portray thoughts and feelings through a character's eyes.

Mrs. G.: We have been working on creating characters. As a part of that process, writers create something called *voice*. The voice is the narrator's personality or a character's personality that shines through in the writing. This can be easily seen in first-person narrated stories. For example, who is the narrator in *From the Mixed-Up Files of Mrs. Basil E. Frankweiler?*

Brachie: Mrs. Frankweiler.

Mrs. G: Good. It's her voice we hear as we read this book. What do you think the author does to portray the first-person narrator's voice?

Sara: She shows us the narrator's thoughts and feelings. Like her way of thinking and what she notices.

Mrs. G.: Yes. The way she thinks and reacts to events help create her voice. Today we are going to concentrate on how authors create strong voice with their first-person narrator characters. I will read the first few pages of *Earrings* by Judith Viorst. Listen for how the author depicts the main character's voice.

NOTE: My students are already familiar with the texts used in mini-lessons, so we are revisiting the books to analyze craft. In this story a young girl is begging her parents to let her have pierced ears so she can wear beautiful earrings.

> I want them.
> I need them.
> I love them.
> I've got to have them.
> —from *Earrings* by Judith Viorst

After I read aloud, students share their observations:

Leah: She lists her feelings in a way that shows her personality. "I want…I need…"

The voice is demanding.

Rachel: She focuses on one thing that she wants: earrings.

Mrs. G.: Good points. We talked earlier about character tags as one trait. With this character, the author focuses the whole narrative around the main character's desire for earrings.

Suggested Books

✗ *Alexander and the Terrible, Horrible, No Good, Very Bad Day* by Judith Viorst

A Bargain for Frances by Russell Hoban

✗ *Charlotte's Web* by E. B. White

Childtimes by Eloise Greenfield and Lessie Jones Little

The Chocolate Touch by Patrick Skene Catling

"Clothes" by Jean Little from *Hey World, Here I Am!*

Earrings by Judith Viorst

"Eleven" by Sandra Cisneros

Fireflies by Julie Brinckloe

Harriet, You'll Drive Me Wild by Mem Fox

Harriet's Recital by Nancy Carlson

Hope's Crossing by Joan Elizabeth Goodman

Jamaica's Find by Juanita Havill

My Rotten, Redheaded Older Brother by Patricia Polacco

The Picture by Catherine Brighton

Princess Pearl by Nicki Weiss

The Relatives Came by Cynthia Rylant

Ruby the Copycat by Peggy Rathmann

Thundercake by Patricia Polacco

Miri: She keeps asking in a demanding way, and she exaggerates, like when she says, "I have to have them." And she says, "Beautiful earrings. Glorious earrings."

Mrs. G.: So what she says and how she says it, meaning her vocabulary and way of speaking, creates voice. She uses the word *glorious*. Not every girl would use that word.

Dina: She keeps repeating that she wants them and needs them and how beautiful pierced earrings are.

Mrs. G.: Notice that she speaks in short sentences. Does that help create her voice?

Dina: She doesn't give up, and she's nagging.

Avigail: She exaggerates when she says, "I am the only girl in the solar system."

Etti: She's so impatient.

Mrs. G.: Yes. The short sentences make her seem energetic.

I list the following ideas on our chart:

How Authors Portray Voice

I. The extent to which an author shares her thoughts, her feelings

2. The kinds of events and feelings the character focuses on

3. The words she uses—words can convey age, a flair for melodrama, a fun-loving nature, a thoughtful nature, and so on

4. How character says things (tempo—length of sentences)

Next, I share a few passages from Sandra Cisneros' short story, "Eleven." This is a short, personal narrative about a girl's experience in school on her eleventh birthday. Rachel's teacher mistakenly assumes an ugly red sweater belongs to Rachel, and the teacher forces her to put it on. Just as in *Earrings*, here, too, the author evokes feelings in the reader because she writes with a strong voice. I ask students to share favorite examples of the narrator's voice.

Michal: In the beginning when she says, "Only today I wish I didn't have only eleven years rattling inside me like pennies in a tin Band-Aid box. Today I wish I was one hundred and two instead of eleven."

Mrs. G.: I like what Michal chose. The narrator shows just how strongly she laments turning eleven by saying she'd rather be one hundred and two. What about the use of a simile? "…like pennies in a tin Band-Aid box." How does that contribute to the voice and our sense of the character?

Aliza: She tells her feelings in her own way.

Mrs. G: She's sensitive, writerly, isn't she?

Aliza: Yeah. Also, when she says: "Its an ugly sweater with red plastic buttons and a collar and sleeves all stretched out like you could use it for a jump rope. It's maybe a thousand years old and even if it belonged to me I wouldn't say so."

Mrs. G.: How does the author portray the narrator's voice here?

Aliza: She shows her feelings and she exaggerates to make her point.

Mrs. G.: Yes. Her personality shines through in the words she chooses. Any other places?

Dina: When she says, "That's not. I don't, you're not. . . Not mine." She can't get her words out. The sentences are short and interrupted. That shows she's shy and afraid to say her feelings.

Mrs. G.: Dina noticed the sentence structure and the cadence of her voice—the rhythm of her words. She spoke in short, interrupted sentences, which showed she was shy and upset. Good. You've all shared great examples of strong voice, and pointed out the various ways the author got that voice across. Now I want you to experiment with putting voice into a notebook entry by writing as the first-person narrator. Writing with strong voice will help you to create strong characters in your stories.

The students work on their entries immediately following the mini-lesson. Here are a few examples. Feel free to share these—or any other student writing in this book—with your students.

Leave Me Alone

Me myself and I
I want to be alone
Leave me alone!!!
I want to sit on a rock
and be alone
   me
   myself
   and I

               —by Ariel, grade 5

In Ariel's piece, the narrator tells her feelings and thoughts, and she uses repetition for emphasis. Her short sentences—some lines are just one word—with repetition create an insistent voice. She's someone who needs privacy, and she expresses her feelings directly.

The Last Piece of Cake

Whoever ate the last piece of cake made
a very big mistake. Whoever ate the
last piece of cake shall never get another piece. Whoever ate the last piece
of cake shall be grounded for three years. Whoever ate the last piece of
cake should be ashamed. What's that you said? I ate the last piece of cake.
Oops! My mistake.

               —by Ariel, grade 5

I love the voice in this piece. We definitely get a feeling of the narrator's personality from the way she speaks and exaggerates. She's someone who believes in pursuing justice and who takes things very much to heart. She's also able to admit when she's wrong with a good sense of humor, as indicated by the last line.

Exploring Voice in Literature

When teaching students about voice in writing, sharing models from literature is the best way to open up kids to different types of voices. In the course of a mini-lesson, I often share three or four passages, drawing from various books.

First, I read an example of a grandmother speaking:

> It's been a good long time since my childtime. Yours is now, you're living your childtime right this minute, but I've got to go way, way back to remember mine.
>
> Memory is a funny thing. You never know how it's going to act. A lot of things that I saw and heard and heard about, when I was a girl, I can't call to mind at all now. My memory just hop-skips right over them. Some other things, I can almost remember, but when I try to catch hold of them, they get mixed up with something else, or disappear. But then, there are the things that keep coming back, keep coming back just as plain, just as clear...

> —from *Childtimes* by Eloise Greenfield and Lessie Jones Little

Mrs. G.: How would you describe her voice?

Chani: She sounds like she's from the South the way she says "childtime."

Miriam: She uses different expressions like "hop-skips." I think she's creative.

Mrs. G.: Does she sound thoughtful or serious or happy?

Devora: She sounds like she's thoughtful. She's remembering her childhood, and she's thinking about how her memory isn't working so well now.

Mrs. G.: I feel like I can actually hear her talking from the words she chooses, like "childtimes" or "I can't call to mind," and from the rhythm of her sentences. She speaks in a slow tempo like an older person. "I've got to go way, way back to remember mine." Notice how she repeats "keep coming back." As if she's thinking of something as she says it.

Next, I read a different type of voice:

> I went to sleep with gum in my mouth and now there's gum in my hair and when I got out of bed this morning I tripped on the skateboard and by mistake I dropped my sweater in the sink while the water was running and I could tell it was going to be a terrible, horrible, no good, very bad day.

> —from *Alexander and the Terrible, Horrible, No Good, Very Bad Day* by Judith Viorst

Mrs. G.: What do you notice about this character's word choice and how he speaks?

Naomi: He exaggerates, like when he says it's going to be a terrible, horrible, no good, very bad day. He talks in long running sentences, like he's in a hurry to tell his feelings.

Mrs. G.: Good. It does sound like he's talking without a breath to pour out his feelings. You noticed the cadence or rhythm of how his words flow.

Talia: From the examples he told we see he lets little things get him upset.

Next, I read this passage:

> They came one moonless night in November. The dogs heard them and set to barking, but no one who could save us was there to hear. I had woken before our dogs, knowing something was terribly wrong. My first thoughts were for Father, gone a fortnight on General Washington's orders. Was he in danger? Had he been wounded? Or was it Mother? She'd been so low since the birth of Jonathan. With the sudden departure of Father, her spirits had sunk further. Was she worse? And the babe, himself so small and weak, had he sickened? Until Jack and Jubal started barking I'd had no fears for myself.

—from *Hope's Crossing* by Joan Elizabeth Goodman

Mrs. G.: What do you notice about the main character's word choice and her feelings?

Leah: Her way of speaking is from very long ago. She says, "set to barking" and the "babe." Also, you see she's very mature because she worries about her parents and their situations before her own.

Mrs. G.: You noticed her sentence structure, which reflected that she was living during the Revolutionary War. Yes, from what she says, we see that she cares very much about her family.

Dina: She seems brave the way she feels something is wrong, but she had no fears for herself.

Mrs. G.: Notice her word choice. She describes the night as moonless. She's poetic. She thinks through all different possibilities, which shows she's intelligent and reflective. What about the rhythm or how her sentences flow?

Esti: She talks in rhythmic sentences. "I had woken before our dogs, knowing something was terribly wrong. My first thoughts were for Father, gone a fortnight on General Washington's orders…"

A WRITER'S INSIGHT

"Your choice of words that your character speaks is one of your best means of characterizing him. No two people use the same words and with the same frequency or in the same arrangement….The speed with which a character talks and the spacing or pace of his words and sentences are sound indexes to your actor as a person."

—Maren Elwood

Partners Find Voice in Picture Books

Have students work in pairs to mark with sticky notes examples of strong voice in a first-person narrator picture book or short text. Some suggested titles: *Thundercake* by Patricia Polacco; *My Rotten, Redheaded Older Brother* by Patricia Polacco; "Clothes" (*Hey World, Here I Am!*) by Jean Little; "Hair" (*The House on Mango Street*) by Sandra Cisneros.

Allowing the Reader to Envision

GOAL: *To explore what the author wants you to infer about character—learning to spot "white spaces"*

"Readers may pay little attention to physical description, preferring to fill in the physical details of the characters in whom they are interested out of their own imagination and tastes.

—Oakley Hall

When my mother, who is an artist, creates a painting, she never covers every inch of canvas. She leaves white spaces to accent the color. The same idea holds true for a writer. A writer knows her character thoroughly, but doesn't need to portray every detail of her knowledge. She leaves white spaces for the reader to envision, to infer. The details that are left out nonetheless inform and accent the traits the reader sees. One of the joys of reading involves bringing our own imagination to the text, to "read between the lines."

To teach this "white spaces" concept to children, I spend four or five days on it. I teach the first mini-lesson with follow-up writing for two days and then the interview lessons (page 56) and related lessons (page 58) for two or three days, depending on the pace of the students.

Part One: *Revisit the Character Tag Sheet*

In the beginning of our character study, I asked students to think of a trait or tag for their character. Now I want them to move beyond this. Together we use one of the student's character tag sheets (see page 38) in a whole-class lesson and we brainstorm a list of additional traits for that character. For example, in Chani and Talia's "The Little White Rabbit" (page 36), the tag was that he is shy. Chani and Talia elaborate that he is clumsy, very beautiful, loves his family, doesn't like parties, and likes to jump and move fast. Other students offer ideas as well.

> **Mrs. G.:** Now that we have brainstormed this list of additional characteristics for the white rabbit, I have a surprise: Chani and Talia might not use all of them for their story. Some details would remain in their heads, informing them as they revise the story, but they wouldn't have to be directly stated in it. You know how an artist often leaves white spaces or parts of the canvas plain, so she doesn't cover the whole surface with color? The white spaces add to the painting by accenting the colors. Writers leave white spaces for the reader, too. Not knowing every detail about the character sparks the reader's imagination, and that adds to the reader's enjoyment.

Part Two: *Look at Picture Books*

Mrs. G.: To show you how a writer uses this technique, I am going to read you *The Relatives Came* by Cynthia Rylant. Listen for the white spaces—the parts the author leaves to our imaginations. [I read aloud the book.] Okay, who has some to share? I'll write your ideas on chart paper, so we can see the kinds of details this author invites us to visualize for ourselves.

Etti: It doesn't say what they are eating at the barbecue.

Mrs. G.: You have to imagine that.

Sprintzy: It doesn't give any of their names.

Faiga: You don't know how they are related.

Bina: You don't know all the things they did together.

Faiga: On the last page you don't know who that lady is in the nightdress. I imagine she is tired but it doesn't say that.

Sarah: It doesn't tell much about the people being visited. You don't even know where they live. It tells more about the relatives visiting from Virginia.

Rachel: You don't know how old they are.

Faiga: It says they hug but it doesn't say other things they do.

Mrs. G.: You don't even know all their conversations. You have to imagine some of the things they might talk about together.

Next, I read aloud *The Picture* by Catherine Brighton. This short book depicts a child who is ill. Magically, she enters the picture on the wall in her room. The students share all the details left to the reader's imagination, as they did with the preceding picture book.

Part Three: *Use the White Spaces Reproducible*

Mrs. G.: Now it's your turn to use this technique in your writing. [I hand out the White Spaces reproducible, page 57] I want you to think about the character you created or a new one and fill out some of the details that only you the author knows. Notice there's room for you to add your own questions to the sheet. And you don't have to answer every question. Answer what makes sense for you. When you write your story, you'll decide which details to share with the reader and which details to leave to the reader's imagination.

Partner Activity: *Discuss Characters Before Writing*

The more information students know about their character before they write, the better they will be able to imagine their character and how she will act in the story. To help this process along, have students bounce ideas off a peer after they have filled out their reproducibles. They can take turns talking about their characters. Or, students can do a role-play, during which they each act like their characters. After 15 minutes of this, my students are usually eager to start writing, and use *some* of the information on their White Spaces sheets in their stories. Note: So students aren't tempted to overload their stories with ideas from the sheet, suggest they leave out at least two characteristics. This helps students grasp that authors are supposed to know more information about their characters than they ever reveal in the text.

Here is Sara Rachel's White Spaces sheet for her story "Rosemary." In her final piece, she includes her character's favorite book and food, but leaves out the character's wishes, her least favorite thing, favorite color and favorite clothing, and details about her family. Those things were left to the reader's imagination.

Student name: _____ Date: _____

White Spaces: Facts I Know About My Character

My character looks like _____.

My character's favorite food is _Cotton candy_____

My character's favorite color is _____aqua_____

My character's favorite clothes are _sweatshirts and button down skirts_

My character's least favorite thing is _School and spinach_____

My character's favorite book is _Harry Potter_____

My character's family is _____

The main thing my character looks for in a friend is _humor_____

My character worries about _____

My character wishes that _____

Goes to popular girls birthday party | Crushes into everything during the whole meal | Laughs and says she's sorry everyone

Other information about my character: _____ | laughs and forgives her.

Memorable Characters...Magnificent Stories Scholastic Professional Books   57

BUILDING ON THE MINI-LESSON:

Interviews

An interview is a good genre to demonstrate white spaces. The interviewer will gather much more information than she will actually be able to put into her published interview.

In the following activity, students interview a book character, and in so doing, gain a sharper sense of what traits an author included in the story—and what was left unsaid.

First, have students choose a character from a class novel or independent book they've recently read. Ask them to brainstorm and write a list of questions about the character; the questions should arise from information found in the text. Next, have students choose a partner to give the list of questions to so he or she can act as interviewer. Now, pretending he or she is the character, the student answers questions posed by the interviewer, elaborating with what he or she imagines about the character (white spaces). Then have students switch roles.

Example: An interview with the character Claudia from *The Mixed-Up Files of Mrs. Basil E. Frankweiler* by E. L. Konigsburg:

Interviewer: Tell us something about yourself.

Claudia: I like things clean. I have three brothers, and they don't have to do as many chores as me (from the text).

Interviewer: What do you look for in a good friend?

Claudia: I like someone who loves adventure and who is sensitive to people's feelings (a white spaces answer).

56

Student name: _____ Date: _____

White Spaces: Facts I Know About My Character

My character looks like _____.

My character's favorite food is _____.

My character's favorite color is _____.

My character's favorite clothes are _____.

My character's least favorite thing is _____.

My character's favorite book is _____.

My character's family is _____.

The main thing my character looks for in a friend is _____.

My character worries about _____.

My character wishes that _____.

Other information about my character: _____

_____.

Special Guest

To add extra excitement to writing an interview using white spaces, I present a special guest to the classroom. Especially with the younger students, a surprise guest builds delicious suspense until she finally appears. My surprise guest is a gawky bird marionette made of white feathers with a blue feather on her head and wobbly, long legs. (Any colorful, interesting puppet will do.) I ask students to describe the puppet. We also have fun brainstorming a name for her. We make a list of adjectives. (This is a good opportunity to teach or to reinforce the concept of adjectives.) Then, together, we come up with a list of interview questions for the puppet. I explain how good interview questions elicit a story and I model a few good questions as examples. In pairs or by themselves, students write the answers to the interview questions using their imaginations to create the puppet's personality. Next, they write a story about the puppet using information from the interview and leaving some information to the reader's imagination.

Mrs. Garber with the bird marionette

Some Interview Questions for Our Parrot Puppet

How do you feel about flying? Tell us about your flight here.

Do you have a favorite thinking place? Where is it and why do you like it?

What's your favorite quiet activity?

What's your favorite noisy activity?

What's your least favorite thing to do?

Who's your best friend and why?

What do you want to be when you grow up and why?

What gift would you like for your birthday?

If you had one wish that could come true what would you wish?

Tell about your first day of "bird school" this year or your very first day in "bird kindergarten."

Analyzing How Writers Use White Spaces in the Class-Shared Novel and Other Texts

Finding the "white spaces" becomes a fun activity using the independent books and other books we read during the year. It helps children think more deeply about the characters they create in their own writing. During our 25-minute independent reading period, I ask students to use sticky notes to mark examples of white spaces in the novels. We do this each day while studying white spaces, which usually takes four to five days. At the end of each independent reading session, I usually ask children to share one or two of their white spaces sticky notes with the class.

CHAPTER 4

Opposites Attract

Teaching Students How to Use Contrasting Characters to Create Dynamic Plots

Fifth graders share their writing at a local bookstore.

THE MINI-LESSONS	THE GOALS
Contrast Builds Conflict	To chart contrast between the protagonist and the antagonist
Experimenting With Point of View	To analyze why authors use different points of view

Contrast Builds Conflict

GOAL: *To chart contrast between the protagonist and the antagonist*

"Without counterpoint there is no harmony."
—Lajos Egri

Now we are ready to add another dimension to our character-building study. I introduce the tool of contrast, which writers use to highlight character traits and to create conflict, which is also called dramatic tension. Playwrights, novelists, television writers, and movie writers use this "opposites attract" device all the time. Think of Shakespeare's Romeo and Juliet from feuding families or *West Side Story*'s Maria and Tony from different backgrounds and also feuding sides. Or the main characters in *Sense and Sensibility* by Jane Austen—Mariane Dashwood is passionate and emotional and her sister, Elinor is reserved and disciplined. Finally, think about *Charlotte's Web* with Charlotte who is controlled and brave and Wilbur who is emotional and frightened. In each of these examples, the characters have opposite traits that draw them to each other.

Here is how I launch the mini-lesson:

Mrs. G.: Authors use a tool called *contrast* when they create characters. What is contrast?

Rachel: Showing differences?

Mrs.G.: Yes. What do you think "contrasting characters" means?

Rina: Making characters with opposite traits?

Mrs. G.: Yes. Can you think of two characters in our class novel that have opposite traits?

Mindy: In *From the Mixed-Up Files of Mrs. Basil E. Frankweiler*, Jamie and Claudia are opposites.

Mrs. G.: Explain that more.

Mindy: Jamie is messy, and he is a miser about money, and Claudia is super-neat. She says she can't imagine not bathing every day and changing her underwear. She wants to spend money more, and she would take a bus instead of walking.

Miriam: Claudia likes to study and Jamie doesn't. She wants to learn all the information in the Metropolitan Museum.

Chaya: Claudia likes things organized and safe. Jamie likes adventures and complications. Like when he tried to eat the note she gave him.

Mrs. G.: So why do you think the author uses contrast between the characters? How does it add to the story?

Suggested Books

Ben and Me by Robert Lawson

Charlotte's Web by E. B. White

The Chocolate Touch by Patrick Skene Catling

Degas and the Little Dancer by Laurence Anholt

From the Mixed-Up Files of Mrs. Basil T. Frankweiler by E. L. Konigsburg

Miss Nelson is Missing by Harry Allard and James Marshall

Number the Stars by Lois Lowry

The Pain and the Great One by Judy Blume

The Talking Eggs by Robert D. San Souci

Chava: It makes them get into fights. I guess it causes problems.

Mrs. G.: Good, it creates conflict. What else?

Michal: It makes each one look stronger. Jamie seems more stingy about money, and Claudia more neat and clean because Jamie isn't.

Mrs. G.: Exactly. The contrast accents, or highlights, each character's traits. It's like a dark background in a painting with light color. The dark background highlights the light color. In some of the picture books I read you this year, the main character contrasted with the other characters. Can you think of an example?

Tali: Madeline was different from the other girls. She was adventurous, and also she was the smallest. She was the leader.

Mrs. G.: Good point.

Dina: Ferdinand was different than the other bulls. He only liked to sit and smell the flowers. He was gentle. He wasn't rough and mean like the other bulls, who liked to fight.

Mrs. G.: How does this lead to conflict?

Dina: Ferdinand is not a fighter so it causes problems when they take him to the bullring in Madrid.

Mrs. G.: Great, you're all on target. Now I am going to read you a book with contrasting characters, *Miss Nelson Is Missing!* by Harry Allard and James Marshall. In this book the author contrasts sweet, soft-spoken Miss Nelson to witchy, loud, no-nonsense Viola Swamp, the substitute. While I read, note contrasts between the two main characters.

The following is a list of characteristics the class composed:

Viola Swamp	Miss Nelson
mean	sweet
strict	not strict
nasty	kind
grumpy	cheerful
ugly	pretty
hooked nose	
dark dress	light dress
dark hair	light hair
controls class	wild class
no story hour	story hour
hates children	likes children
impatient	patient
name: Viola Swamp sounds means	name: Miss Nelson sounds nice

BUILDING ON THE MINI-LESSON:

Writing Notebook Entries About Contrasting Characters

Next, I ask students to use the Contrasting Characters Chart reproducible (see page 63) to help plan for contrast between two characters in new stories they write. After students fill out the chart, I guide them to write stories that use these contrasts to fuel the story line. Contrasting personalities often clash, which makes for dynamic plots. As students work on their stories, I continue to model how authors use both contrasting characters and character tags to create story conflict.

Charting the Contrasts of Book Characters

Have pairs of students look through their independent reading books or the shared class novel and identify main characters that seem to contrast with one another. Next, have them list these differing traits on the Contrasting Characters Chart reproducible. As they skim the book, have them write on sticky notes evidence of these traits in the text, and examples of when these contrasts lead to problems, scenes of conflict, and so on. This activity also effectively lays the ground work for writing literary essays on contrasting characters. Students can also use the Contrasting Characters Chart to explore the differences between two characters in two different texts.

Name: _____ Date: _____

Contrasting Characters Chart

Character's name: **Character's name:**

_____   _____

Contrasting Traits

Some conflicts that might arise because of their differences:

_____

_____

_____

Events in the plot that would show these conflicts:

_____

_____

_____

Fifth-grader Baila explores the contrasts between Annemarie and Ellen in *Number the Stars* **by Lois Lowry.**

Ellen has dark hair and Annemarie has blonde hair. Ellen is Jewish and Annemarie is Danish, page 1.

Ellen is stocky while Annemarie is tall and lanky. "She was a stocky ten-year old, unlike lanky Annemarie." (Because of this, Annemarie is a good runner, unlike Ellen, page 1.)

Annemarie tries to make them feel better by lying, unlike Ellen who actually solves the problem with her cleverness. (Ellen solves Kirsti's shoe problem, while Annmarie just lies, page 29.)

Annemarie just plays with Kirsti to stop her from pestering, but Ellen really cares about Kirsti. (Ellen lets Kirsti play dolls, page 30.)

Annemarie knows how to act in the time of danger, but Ellen doesn't act quick enough. (When Ellen's necklace is stuck, Annemarie pulls it off, page 45.)

Independent Activity: *Venn Diagrams to Show Contrast*

Invite students to compare characters in different texts using a Venn diagram. Students list character traits of two characters in two large circles that overlap. They list character traits that they have in common in the middle circle. For example, in the sample at right, students compared the doctor characters from two different texts: *Charlotte's Web* and *The Chocolate Touch*.

Following is a sample of student writing after the mini-lesson. First, Esti filled out the Contrasting Characters Chart as a prewriting warm-up (see sample, below). Then, she used the information to write her story, "The Big Twins." Later, she published it as a picture book.

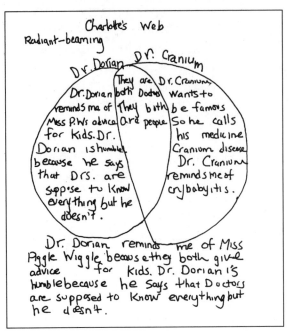

Contrast Chart

Character's Name   **Character's Name**

Teeny   **Contrasting Traits**   Weeny

1. outgoing   1. shy
2. loves to play sports   2. loves to read + write
3. Messy   3. clean
4.   4.

The Big Twins

Our names are Teeny and Weeny Big. We are twins. We are not identical. Our clothes are not identical. But our smiles are. We sit next to each other in class. I, Teeny, love to play sports. I am also very outgoing.

Hi. I am Weeny. I love to read and write. I am very shy. I am very, very clean. I am very messy. Hey Teeny. This is my page.

I don't care.

Well, you should. Anyway, as I was saying. I am very neat and clean. I am very tired now. I have to go to sleep. Bye-bye. Now here comes Teeny again.

One day when we came home from school, Mommy said, "I just got a call from your teacher. She said that you two always have the same things wrong and the same wrong answers. She said that she can tell by tests and class sheets that Teeny is copying Weeny's homework. She said either way that Weeny will have to go to sixth grade or Teeny will have to go to fourth grade."

We didn't say anything. We ran to our room. Weeny said, "I know you would be embarrassed since we know some girls in fourth grade. But I will not fit in sixth grade. I'm not their level. I usually get 95 percent in fifth grade. In sixth grade, I'll probably get a 85 percent. "Listen," I said. "Why don't we ask for one more chance. We won't do homework together."

"Good idea," she said.

We asked our teacher. She said, "Okay."

We never did homework together again. Just once in a while... One day our teacher said, "You may both stay."

    —by Esti, grade 5

Experimenting With Point of View

GOAL: *To analyze why authors use different points of view*

"Often the most important decision a writer will have to make in a piece of fiction is how the point of view is to be handled. The imprint of a point of view contributes enormously to the process of dramatization and the way detail is viewed contributes in turn to the characterization of the viewpoint character."

—Oakley Hall

Authors may choose to tell a story from many different points of view. Authors decide on whose point of view they will tell the story based on the effect they wish to achieve. First-person stories have the "I" telling the story. In a third-person story, the narrator/author tells the story using "he" or "she" to refer to the characters. Many authors use the limited third person, which means they tell the story from one particular character's viewpoint using the "he" or "she" pronoun. An omniscient observer sees everything that happens. Shifting viewpoint means the author shifts to different characters telling the story.

To begin our discussion, I have students think about the stories they've read and categorize each story's point of view.

Mrs. G.: Authors tell stories from a certain point of view. For example, in "The Three Little Pigs," the wolf doesn't tell the story. It's told from the pigs' perspective. What are some possible points of view?

Michal: "I" stories.

Mrs. G.: Good. [I write "First person" on the chart paper.] Can you think of an example of a first-person story?

Michal: *Earrings.*

Mrs. G.: Who tells the story in that book?

Michal: The main character. The girl who wants earrings, but it never tells you her name.

Mrs. G.: Why does this first-person point of view seem just right for the story?

Leah: Because the main character's voice comes through strongly. She says her feelings, and it's her story.

Mrs. G.: I agree that in this book the story comes out stronger with the main character telling it. Can you think of another book written in a first-person point of view?

Raizy: *Hope's Crossing.*

Mrs. G.: Why is the first-person point of view right for that book?

Dina: It's all about what happens to Hope. So if it wasn't told by her you wouldn't know all the things that happened and what she thought and felt about them.

Mrs. G.: It could be told in the third person, but I agree that it makes the book stronger to have Hope tell directly the story of what happens to her after she is kidnapped during the Revolutionary War. What other points of view do authors use?

Etti: "He" or "she."

Mrs. G.: Good, that's called third person. There is also third-person limited when you see the whole story through one character's eyes. Can you think of an example of that?

Etti: *Charlotte's Web* is through Wilbur's eyes.

Mrs. G.: Why do you think E. B. White chose this type of point of view instead of first person?

Miri: He tells about Fern and about Charlotte, and he wouldn't be able to do it the same way if it wasn't all told by Wilbur.

Mrs. G.: Good point. When the story is in first person you are limited to that one character's thoughts and feelings. You can't describe scenes when that character isn't there.

Now, let's create examples of the kinds of point of view, so we have a reference chart when we go to write our own stories. [We create a chart like the one on page 69.]

Mrs. G.: Now, think about *From the Mixed-Up Files of Mrs. Basil E. Frankweiler.* Why do you think E. L. Konigsburg chose Mrs. Frankweiler to tell the story instead of Claudia or James?

Etta: Well, this way she knew things, like how her parents put an ad in the paper and other stuff they wouldn't know. Except, couldn't she have told it from the parents' point of view?

Mrs. G.: What problem would there be if she chose their viewpoint?

Michal: They wouldn't know everything that happened in the museum.

Etta: They could have told it after it happened.

Mrs. G.: You mean like a flashback. That's true.

Looking at More Picture Books

Next, I read aloud *The Pain and the Great One* by Judy Blume. This picture book depicts the feelings of a younger brother and his older sister toward one another. I explain that Judy Blume probably chose a shifting point of view because she wanted to show both sides of the brother and sister relationship. In this lesson I ask students to look for the differences in viewpoint when the sister and brother tell the story. I tell them that when they write, they must think about who is telling the story.

I also share other books told from a unique point of view. *Degas and the Little Dancer* by Laurence Anholt is the story of the famous little dancer statue that Degas created. Marie wants more than anything to become a famous ballet dancer. She progresses in her ballet studies, but her father falls ill. She must earn money to help pay his doctor bills. Degas

First Person

The story is told by one character. He narrates the story.

EXAMPLE: I, David Small, took a trip to see the Grand Canyon with my nephews, Mark and Ken. The canyon was magnificent at sunrise and sunset.

Third Person

The story is told by a narrator. In third person limited, the story is told from one particular character's viewpoint, using the "he" and "she" pronouns.

EXAMPLE: David Small took a trip to the Grand Canyon with his nephews, Mark and Ken. David found the canyon magnificent. His nephews, one of whom was afraid of heights, weren't as awed.

Shifting Viewpoints

The author shifts points of view between two or more characters.

EXAMPLE: Magnificent!, David thought, taking a picture of the canyon bathed in the splendid reds and gold of sunset.

A few steps behind him, Mark turned himself away from the view, and patted the nose of the donkey, still feeling queasy from gazing down near the edge. He looked at his brother Ken and said, "I wish I had our uncle's nerve."

Omniscient

The author establishes a narrator wholly outside the story, who can get inside the head of every character's thoughts, and can describe all the events. An omniscient narrator is all-knowing.

EXAMPLE: "It was the best of times. It was the worst of times..."

— *A Tale of Two Cities*, Charles Dickens

offers her a job to pose. He creates the statue that makes her the most famous dancer in the world. The author uses an outside narrator, the museum guard, to tell the story.

Mrs. G.: What other possible viewpoints could he have chosen?

Dina: The statue or the girl, Marie.

Raina: Someone visiting the museum.

Shani: The artist, Degas.

Shira: Another dancer in the company.

Mrs. G.: Writers have many possible viewpoints from which to choose. They choose the viewpoint which will best tell the particular story they have in their head. Why do you think the author chose the museum guard to tell the story?

Leora: He can describe more because he is with the statue every day, and he knows her well.

Rivka: He can go back and forth in time. Marie wouldn't know about our time period today in the museum.

Tova: He was outside the story so he could tell it.

Mrs. G.: Good. *From the Mixed-Up Files of Mrs. Basil E. Frankweiler* also has someone outside of the story telling the story, although toward the end she does become a character in the story.

BUILDING ON THE MINI-LESSON:

Try Writing From a Different Viewpoint

After our conversation, I invite students to experiment writing notebook entries from interesting viewpoints or to rewrite existing entries from another point of view.

Here are some examples:

> The people were running
> To safety.
> A white wave cascaded down the mountain. The people almost thought they
> Were goners, when
> The little girl calmly closed her bottle of glue.
> —by Chana M., grade 6

This entry delightfully surprises the reader. When I read it aloud to classes, there is always a pause followed by, "Oh, I get it!' Students love the twist at the end. The following entries were inspired by Chana's.

Bubble Gum

Help! Help! The city is turning pink!
A balloon is going to explode. The whole city is exploding! Until the little boy popped his bubble gum bubble into his mouth.
—by Shoshana, grade 3

Shoshana also crafted a surprise twist involving the point of view.

Oh, What a Horror to Live in the Barber's Shop

What a horror to live in the barber's shop. Snip, Snip, Snip
All day long, hair drops on the floor like rain drops down your window pane.
—by Kayla, grade 3

Kayla's intriguing entry makes me wonder who is telling the story. She sets up an interesting setting and character feelings. We want to hear more. These forays into point of view really help students to loosen up their writing, and to experiment. The goal of each of the mini-lessons in this book is to help students produce writing that surprises and intrigues, and make us think anew with its insight. We don't want a classroom full of writers who feel they have to play it safe.

On the following page is a reproducible that gives students structure as they consider point of view for their stories. Note that I didn't include omniscient as this viewpoint is very difficult for students to use.

Point of View: Try It Out

First Person

Try a few lines of descriptions using "I". Will this work for the whole story? Is there a part where the "I" won't be there and you need to describe something?

_____

_____

_____

_____

_____

Third Person

Try a few lines using "he" or "she".

_____

_____

_____

_____

_____

Shifting Viewpoint

Try a few lines shifting the point of view. Does this work well for your story? Do we need different people's viewpoints to make the story work?

_____

_____

_____

_____

_____

CHAPTER 5

So What Have You Learned, Dorothy?

Teaching Students How to Build Character Growth Into Their Stories

Third-grade students display their published work and an About-the-Author booklet.

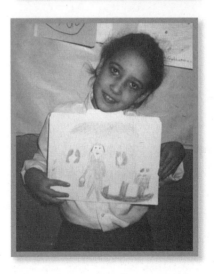

THE MINI-LESSON	THE GOAL
Change and Growth in Characters	To pinpoint places in books and student writing where characters change

Change and Growth in Characters

GOAL: *To pinpoint places in books and student writing where characters change*

"The only thing that one really knows about human nature is that it changes. Change is the one quality we can predicate of it. The systems that fail are those that rely on the permanency of human nature, and not its growth and development."

—Oscar Wilde

Everybody knows the scene in Frank L. Baum's classic *The Wizard of Oz*—or Hollywood's version of it—when the Tin Man turns and says, "So what have you learned, Dorothy?" to which the homesick heroine replies, "If you go searching for something and it's not in your own backyard, you probably never really lost it to begin with."

In the best of novels, characters grow and change, and readers witness and empathize with this journey of self-discovery (or in some cases, self-destruction). These moments of revelation are called *epiphanies* and in novels they're often tidier than the more messy or unfinished moments of insight we have in real life. Regardless, without some degree of epiphany, a novel usually falls flat. The characters seem static, and we close the book feeling cheated, as though we invested lots of our time but the author didn't give us enough pay-off, enough insight—about the characters, about human nature, and in turn about ourselves.

Now that students understand how to build story conflict (using story tags and/or contrasting characters), and they've experimented with white spaces, voice, and point of view, they are ready for the next step of showing how a character changes or grows. In the following discussion, fifth graders discuss what helps a character to change or grow. I write down their ideas on chart paper.

Esther: What another character says causes the first character to change.

Dina: The character learns a lesson by doing something.

Sprintzy: Growing older, thinking.

Suggested Books

The Chocolate Touch by Patrick Skene Catling

The Hundred Dresses by Eleanor Estes

Princess Pearl by Nicki Weiss

Mrs. Piggle-Wiggle's Magic by Betty MacDonald

My Rotten, Redheaded Older Brother by Patricia Polacco

Pierre by Maurice Sendak

Ruby the Copycat by Peggy Rathmann

Shadow of a Bull by Maia Wojciechowska

Stone Fox by John Gardiner

Thundercake by Patricia Polacco

Chanie: The character notices something or someone helps them.

Miriam: Something difficult happens.

Mindy: An accident could happen, like in this book where a girl broke her leg.

Ariel: A sickness could make someone change.

Hindy: Someone could make up after a fight.

Leah: Someone could feel sorry for someone.

Tamar: A secret could change someone.

Dalia: Practicing.

Mrs. G.: Interesting. Many stories show characters practicing to reach goals and to grow.

Esti: Environment.

Mrs. G.: What do you mean?

Esti: Like if you live in a place where everyone is evil and you act that way, and then when you move where people aren't like that it makes you change.

Mrs. G.: Wow. You thought of so many great possibilities. Think back to the book I read you, *Ruby the Copycat* by Peggy Rathmann. [I hold up the book.] Did the main character change at all? How?

Miriam: She stopped copying because the teacher talked to her.

Mrs. G.: What did the teacher say?

Miriam: She told her to stop copying and be happy with herself. Also, she noticed Ruby was good at hopping. So she asked Ruby to lead everyone in hopping.

Mrs. G.: Which idea on our chart did the author use to cause Ruby to change?

Leah: Someone important talking to the character.

Mrs. G.: [I point to that on the chart.] Notice it was Ruby herself who thought of her talent of hopping and who actually changed herself into a leader.

Next, I read aloud the book, *A Bargain for Frances* by Russell Hoban. In this classic story Frances goes to play with Thelma. Thelma tricks Frances into buying her plastic tea set so Thelma can go buy the tea set Frances really wants. At the end of the story, both characters have changed and their friendship grows stronger.

How Characters Change

◎ Someone important says something to the character that causes the character to reflect on his actions and change his thinking, attitudes, or beliefs about things

◎ What a character does

◎ Growing older, gaining experience and wisdom from that

◎ Thinking

◎ An accident or sickness or the death of someone

◎ A secret

◎ Making up after a fight

◎ Someone models the right way to do something

◎ Environment

◎ Going through hard times

◎ Practicing

Through discussion, the students explore what causes the characters to change. To sum it up and give students direction for their writing I say:

Mrs. G.: So we see there are many possibilities for what causes your character to change or grow. In your own writing, refer back to your character tag sheet and think about what will cause your character to grow or change. Refer to the chart we just made. We listed different factors that help cause a character to change. Use one of these, but remember that whatever starts the change, it is the main character herself who must do the work to earn the change or growth. In *A Bargain for Frances*, each character had to do something herself in order to learn her lesson. In *Ruby the Copycat*, also, Ruby had to find her own talent and then change.

BUILDING ON THE MINI-LESSON:

Writing Notebook Entries That Show Characters Changing

I shared with my class the following highlights of a writing conference:

Mrs. G.: A student chose a tag of lonely for her main character. In the first draft, the main character suddenly started talking and making friends. I asked her what caused the change. The student went back to her notebook and added one sentence that showed the change: *Her mother said four words: "Have confidence in yourself."*

In another story, "Tommy's Bad Mark," the author showed how Tommy slowly worked on changing his study habits, how he practiced math with his mother and then sat down and studied every day.

Both of these characters earned the solution to their problem. They both had strength that helped them to change. Tommy was really a good student and intelligent; the author told us. He had just fallen into bad study habits. The character who was lonely really liked the other girls, and she wanted to be friends with them. Her mother reminded her of the strength she already had. Now we are going to look at how published authors develop character growth.

Creating organic character growth in a story is a difficult for writers of any age, but I've found that my students *can* make headway. The best way to guide them is to share examples of character growth in literature. For example, in her book *Number the Stars*, Lois Lowry creates organic growth for her character, Annemarie. In the beginning of the book, Annemarie is portrayed as a loyal friend to Ellen. Her character tag is fear of the soldiers and the war. She doesn't consider herself brave. Yet in the beginning chapter, the reader sees Annemarie has strength she doesn't know she has. To explore this with students, I share an excerpt from the opening scene of the book when Annemarie and her friend are stopped by German soldiers on the street:

"Why are you running?" the harsh voice asked.

His Danish was very poor. Three years, Annemarie thought with contempt. Three years they've been in our country, and still they can't speak our language.

"I was racing with my friend," she answered politely. "We have races at school every Friday, and I want to do well, so I—" Her voice trailed away, the sentence unfinished. Don't talk so much, she told herself. Just answer them, that's all.

As the story unfolds, Annemarie gradually discovers her own inner strength and courage when she's called upon to help her friend and her friend's family escape from Denmark. In the end it is Annemarie who must run through the woods to deliver a vital packet that helps her friend and her friend's family escape.

After discussing the book, and sharing other examples from literature, my students are eager to work on this craft. The following story resulted from this mini-lesson:

Camp Catastrophe

In the camp lunchroom Becky sat while everyone talked and laughed. For the game "Elimination," she just sat on the side and sobbed. Then she wiped off her face to make sure no one knew she was crying. But it didn't matter. No one paid attention to her. They only paid attention to the game. For supper Becky had

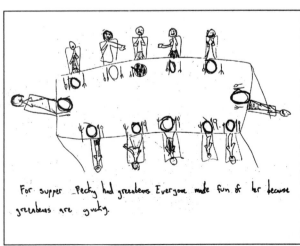

green beans. Everyone made fun of her because green beans are yucky. That night Becky just sobbed, feeling angry at the whole world. The next day was the worst day of Becky's life. Becky called her mother and her mother said only four words. "Have confidence in yourself." All of a sudden, Becky had an idea. All of a sudden she had more confidence in herself. All of a sudden people stopped teasing her. For breakfast Becky ate whatever she wanted and ignored the teasing. In dodge ball Becky hit the ball so hard she got someone out, and she didn't care if she threw the ball a babyish way. She even became friends with Janey, one of the kids in her bunk.

—by Charna, grade 5

Obviously, the point of change in Charna's story was when the mother spoke to Becky and told her to have confidence. As students develop as writers, they will be able to show character change with increasing subtlety and sophistication.

Partners Look for Turning Points in Picture Books

Have students reread familiar picture books and work in pairs to look for the point of change for the main character and identify what causes that change. They can use sticky notes to flag the pages and write comments, then share their findings in a whole-class literary discussion, or in their reading notebooks. Any titles from the book list on page 74 will work well for this activity.

CHAPTER 6

Leora shares her writing with younger students.

Hint, Hint

Teaching Students Simple Ways to Use Foreshadowing

THE MINI-LESSON	THE GOAL
Sprinkling Hints About the Plot Within a Character's Traits	To learn to use foreshadowing

Sprinkling Hints About the Plot Within a Character's Traits

GOAL: *To learn to use foreshadowing*

"Every detail is an omen and cause."

—Jorge Luis Borges

Now that students have worked on crafting character change, they are ready to learn a tool called foreshadowing, in which the author plants hints within the character's actions or within descriptions. Foreshadowing means dropping hints or clues to the reader of events to come. Foreshadowing is just one means of creating suspense. A character's traits can also foreshadow future story events. Writers must carefully place certain details, and these details must reappear later in the text.

In the following mini-lesson, the students and I review a bunch of books we've read, from picture books to novels, and study the various ways authors accomplish foreshadowing.

Mrs. G.: Today we are going to learn about foreshadowing, a technique that helps build suspense. Does anyone know what foreshadowing means?

Leah: A hint from the author?

Mrs. G.: Yes. What smaller words do you notice in the word *foreshadowing*?

Rachel: Shadow. You see a shadow first.

Mrs. G.: Yes. You have *fore* meaning happening before and the word *shadow*. Just as one may see a shadow before a person appears, so the author plants a hint or shadow of something before it appears on the scene.

Authors also use character traits to foreshadow events. *The Ghost-Eye Tree* by Bill Martin Jr. and John Archambault, demonstrates an example of the "smoking-gun" principle. If an author shows a gun on the wall in scene one, by the end of the piece that gun will have to have been used in some way. The scary ghost-eye tree will have to erupt later in the story. Where does the author foreshadow this in the book?

Peri: When the boy says how he dreaded to go, the author is hinting at something that will happen later to prove his fear was not unfounded.

Mrs. G.: The boy's trait of fearfulness foreshadows events in the story.

The boy and girl dance and sing right by the tree, "There's nothing to fear." Here the author foreshadows the opposite of what will happen. A few pages later they run in terror from the ghost-eye tree.

Let's think of another picture book where the author uses foreshadowing with a character's traits. In *Corduroy* by Don Freeman, Corduroy's tag is his need to find his missing button. How is this used as foreshadowing?

Aliza: The first illustration shows Corduroy missing a button. And later he goes to look for it.

Mrs. G.: Good. Can you think of an example of foreshadowing in *Madeline*?

Sarah: Madeline's adventurous streak hints of future events. "And nobody knew so well how to frighten Miss Clavel."

Mrs. G.: Remember the book *Ruby the Copycat* by Peggy Rathmann? Ruby had a trait of being a copycat. How does the author foreshadow events in this book?

Dina: Well, once she copies one of Angela's outfits, you think she'll copy more outfits.

Rachel: And you think she'll copy her poem, too.

Mrs. G.: Good. You all laughed when she stared at the teacher's bright nail polish. Why?

Sprintzy: You knew she would copy her teacher's nails, too.

Mrs. G.: That is an example of a character's trait foreshadowing what will happen. The author also tucked a hint of the solution in Ruby's character. Sprintzy noticed it. I remember she asked, "Why does the author say she hopped?" Think back and you'll see the author sprinkled in Ruby's hopping ability along with other details so we hardly noticed it. Yet Ruby's hopping foreshadows the solution. What was the solution to Ruby's copycatting?

Sprintzy: Ruby can hop, and then everyone will follow her.

Mrs. G.: Also, in *A Bargain for Frances* by Russell Hoban, the author uses another type of foreshadowing technique. Sometimes authors state the opposite of what really will happen. Can you think of a place in the story where someone said something opposite of what really happened?

Shani: When Frances says, "This time I do not have to be careful. We are not playing with boomerangs. We are not skating. We are having a tea party and we are making a mud cake."

Mrs. G.: Good. This statement, which reflects Frances' trusting nature, foreshadows the trouble that comes in the story. Can you think of examples of character traits foreshadowing in our class novel, *Number the Stars* by Lois Lowry?

Raizel: Annemarie is a good runner. Later she will need to run quickly to get the message to her uncle on the boat.

Mrs. G.: The girls run and are stopped by two Nazi soldiers in the beginning. This foreshadows the Nazi's interference in their lives.

Suggested Books

Baby by Patricia MacLachlan

A Bargain for Frances by Russell Hoban

The Ghost-Eye Tree by Bill Martin Jr. and John Archambault

Number the Stars by Lois Lowry

Pierre by Maurice Sendak

Roll of Thunder, Hear My Cry by Mildred Taylor

Ruby the Copycat by Peggy Rathmann

Sarah, Plain and Tall by Patricia MacLachlan

See the Ocean by Estelle Condra

This particular novel often uses the kind of foreshadowing wherein the author has the character state the opposite of what will actually happen. For example, Lois Lowry writes: "Annemarie admitted to herself, snuggling there in the quiet dark, that she was glad to be an ordinary person who would never be called upon for courage." This foreshadows that just the opposite will happen to her.

Foreshadowing is an effective tool because it gives the reader a hint or glimpse that fuels the imagination. When the reader's imagination is sparked, this pulls the reader into the story.

Some of you may be finishing your story or working on publishing it, but some of you may want to try this technique of using character traits to foreshadow events in your story.

BUILDING ON THE MINI-LESSON:

Using Character Traits to Foreshadow Events in Writer's Notebook Entries

I ask students to use the foreshadowing reproducible (see page 84) to list their character's traits and a few events that the traits will foreshadow. I tell them to go ahead and try to tuck some foreshadowing into a new notebook entry or into an existing story. For many students the concept of foreshadowing is taken in a literal way. Often my students place the foreshadowing a few sentences from the event. That is fine. They are learning the idea, and again, constant modeling from good literature scaffolds them toward understanding the use of foreshadowing in a more sophisticated way. I find younger students—especially third and fourth graders—love looking for foreshadowing in their reading or in read-alouds. It's a grown-up concept that they are proud to know. There is definitely a special "I found foreshadowing" shout and joyful smile that I recognize on these students.

The following excerpt from a student entry includes a foreshadowing of a mother's fear of insects and spiders. Later she discovers spiders in her son's suitcase.

Lively Larry

"Larry, did you forget to pack your underwear!?"

"Oops! But Mom, there is no room."

"What? No room? I gave you the biggest bag in the house! How can there be no room? What do you have in there already?"

"A trumpet."

"What? Let's go check it out!"

"Mom, there is nothing in there but my clothes. I really don't think you should

open my suitcase." Larry knew his mother was afraid of insects. Larry was walking through the dining room thinking of what he should get.

"Let's see, three packs of..."

"YAAAAAAAAAAA!"

"What in heaven's earth is in here? SPIDERS? YAAAAAAAA! No wonder you have no room."

"See Mom, I told you not to open my suitcase!"

"Why would you have spiders in there?"

"Well, that is for my private reasons."

Larry was very lively.

　　　　　—by Leeby, grade 5

Finding Examples of Foreshadowing in Novels

I ask students to go back to their independent books to search for character traits that foreshadow events, and to record their findings on the Foreshadowing sheet. Later, they share what they found in a whole-class literary discussion.

Student name: _____ Date: _____

Foreshadowing

My character's name is: _____.

My character's trait that foreshadows is: _____.

List three events that are foreshadowed:

1. _____

2. _____

3. _____

Memorable Characters…Magnificent Stories Scholastic Professional Books

CHAPTER 7

A display of children's memoir book illustrations.

Capturing the Characters in Your Life

Teaching Students How to Fully Sketch People They Know in Memoir Writing

THE MINI-LESSON	THE GOAL
Creating Characters in Memoir	To write memoirs with vivid details and feelings

Creating Characters in Memoir

GOAL: *To write memoirs with vivid details and feelings*

> "The crucial ingredient in memoir is, of course, people. Sounds and smells and songs and sleeping porches will take you just so far. Finally, you must summon back the men and women and children who notably crossed your life. What was it that made them memorable—what turn of mind, what crazy habits?"
>
> —William Zinsser

Beautiful memoir books based on family or personal stories abound in children's literature. I enjoy sharing these books to spark my students' own memoir writing.

Authors create characters from family members like *My Great-Aunt Arizona* by Gloria Houston, which is based on her great-aunt, or *Mirandy and Brother Wind* by Patricia C. McKissack, which is based on her grandparents. Some books like *The Art Lesson* by Tomie dePaola depict the author as a character in a memoir. Writing a memoir ties together lots of things we have worked on previously, such as vivid sensory details, expressing or showing feelings, character tags, contrast, white spaces, foreshadowing, character growth, point of view, and strong character voice.

Mrs. G.: Today we will begin a study of the memoir genre. What word do you notice in the word *memoir*?

Shaina: Memory.

Mrs. G.: Memoir stories can be stories that happened to you or family stories you have heard. Today I am going to read you a memoir by Tomie dePaola about what happened to him when he was a boy. Notice how he portrays feelings and how he tucks details into the text. He shows himself as the main character. Listen for some of the elements we learned about characterization. What's the viewpoint and why? What's his character tag? How does the author create voice? What is the contrast? Listen for moments of foreshadowing and for white spaces.

(In this story Tomie wants more than anything to be an artist. He colors everywhere and waits for first grade when the art lessons will begin in school. The first grade teacher only gives one piece of paper to each student, and she won't let him use his 64 crayons. Tomie lets the art teacher know that he wants to use his own crayons, and he doesn't wish to copy because real artists don't copy.)

After reading aloud, we have the following literary discussion:

Mrs. G.: So what is Tomie's character tag?

Rachel: He loves to color and draw.

Sarah: He wants to be an artist.

Chani: The contrast is that he is the only one who liked to draw and he drew the best of the other kids.

Etta: Also, there is contrast between Mrs. Lander, who is the strict first grade teacher, and Mrs. Bowers, who is the nice art teacher.

Hadassah: It's mean that the art teacher only gives one piece of paper.

Mrs. G.: Yes, that's a detail that sticks in the reader's mind.

Mazal: It's white spaces at the ending because you imagine more and more how he grew up. It doesn't show that part. You just see him grown up on the last page.

Esti: The white space is that he didn't say in the book that it's about himself.

Mrs. G.: What do you mean?

Esti: It says Tomie and so you have to imagine it's talking about Tomie dePaola.

Mrs. G.: What about the point of view? I would have thought that he would have picked first person. Why do you think he chose third person?

Sarala: He couldn't have told the details like how his relatives hung up his pictures and what they thought about them.

Brachie: I like how he talks.

Aliza: It's third person, but we only have Tomie's point of view.

Mrs. G: Good observation. That type of viewpoint is called limited third person because we only see one character's viewpoint in the story.

Mrs. G.: Notice how Tomie shows his feelings when the teacher won't let him keep his 64 crayons in school. He's whispering to his friend in the illustration. He says, "How am I supposed to practice being an artist with SCHOOL CRAYONS?"

Brachie: The change in his character is that he drew better and better.

Suggested Books

- *The Art Lesson* by Tomie dePaola
- *Butterfly* by Patricia Polacco
- "Hair" by Sandra Cisneros
- *Hey World, Here I Am!* by Jean Little
- *Laura Charlotte* by Kathryn O. Galbraith
- "Minit Snowball" by Naomi Shihab Nye
- *Mirandy and Brother Wind* by Patricia C. McKissack
- *My Great-Aunt Arizona* by Gloria Houston
- *My Rotten Redheaded Older Brother* by Patricia Polacco
- *Night in the Country* by Cynthia Rylant
- *The Relatives Came* by Cynthia Rylant
- *Roxaboxen* by Barbara Cooney
- *When I Was Little* by Jamie Lee Curtis
- *Wilfrid Gordon McDonald Partridge* by Mem Fox

Aliza: Also, he was obedient in the beginning, and he stopped coloring on sheets and walls but towards the end he wasn't obedient when he sneaked his box of 64 crayons.

Mrs. G.: Wow. You noticed so many of the elements of characterization.

I shared this short memoir about myself as a young girl.

A Memory

I tear wrapping paper. A furry blue ear pokes out. A blue teddy bear tumbles in my lap. I turn a silver key glistening in his back. Soft tinkling notes sing a melody. I hug him close. A friend to snuggle on cold lonely nights.

Years wind past. He flattens. His blue fur melts to faded love-worn. Each night I hold him, until one day his music stops. As I pat his threadbare stomach, a grown up girl tucks him in her memory.

—by Mrs. Garber

Next I ask students to think of a memory they have from a long time ago or a memory that didn't happen that long ago. I invite them to include sensory details and feelings and to think about conveying voice through word choice, cadence, and tempo—long or short sentences.

The following student memoirs grew from this mini-lesson.

Me and My Grandmother

Every Passover my grandparents come to me. Every morning my grandmother sits in the kitchen with the newspaper and a piece of cake and a cup of coffee. Whenever I come in, I sit down and my grandmother looks up and says, "Good morning." And I repeat, "Good morning." Then she asks if I would like some coffee. And I would say, "Yeah, thank you." And we would sit down together and we eat cake and drink and talk. When me and my grandmother sit down together, I feel warm and cozy. I feel like a sheep so cozy and warm.

—by Atara, grade 5

This short piece conveys strong feelings and a good sense of this student's relationship with her grandmother. Atara includes what she and her grandmother say and do with each other. She gives her grandmother a tag of being hospitable and warm. She leaves white spaces for us to imagine how she and her grandmother look and what else they do together.

My Sister

So loud and annoying
Always copying what I do
Making noise when I'm studying
And starting up with me
But both of us share one personal thing
We have a space in our heart for each other.

—by Pessie, grade 5

Pessie writes with a strong voice. She gives her sister a tag, and she also shows a change in the main character (the narrator) when the narrator thinks deeply about her sister. She uses white spaces for the reader to imagine scenes between the two sisters.

My Mom

My mom is a gift
Everyday I come home
She says, "Mindy, how was your day?"
Every time I go to sleep, she says good night
Whenever she has free time, she spends it with
me. If I'm not there, she reads.
She is such a kind person and mother.
I love her for a lot of things
But most of all I love her for who she is.

—by Mindy, grade 5

This piece also conveys strong feelings and details about this student's mother.

Peaceful Smells

I looked out the window
The wind brushed against my beautiful,
silky blonde hair that always stays in place.
I smelled the peaceful smell of fresh flowers
that just blossomed this spring. I also smelled
a smoky smell of someone barbecuing. I also
smelled Mrs. Baker making luscious chocolate
creamy cupcakes for Shabbos. I also smelled my
mother putting on clear nail polish.

—by Henny, Esty B., Shaindy, and Leora, grade 3

These three girls wrote with strong voice and imagery. The reader can imagine the sensory imagery. This piece seems to foreshadow something special happening with the baking and the mother putting on nail polish.

My Dog

A long time ago I used to have a dog. I had him for six months.
I had to give him away because my mother was sick before we got him,
and when we got him she became even more sick.
I was really sad. I did not stop crying for two hours.
I still miss him. My mother was very sorry. She said when
we move to a house with a backyard we will get me two dogs.
Because when we had him, he would cry because he was lonely
when we would go to school or work.

   —by Natalie, grade 3

Little Details About My Dog

My dog's name was Sparky because his eyes were sparkly.
He was eleven weeks old when we got him. He
was a mutt (a mix of different kinds of dogs).
Once we went to an amusement park and police paged us
because they heard him cry.

This memoir has strong voice and Natalie conveys details about her dog, Sparky. She gives him a tag of crying when he is lonely.

Natalie shares her "Rose" memoir

BUILDING ON THE MINI-LESSON:

Creating Characters Based on Family Stories

On another day, I continue our exploration of memoir by telling students how authors often base stories or books on stories about people in their family. They create the characters based on the people they knew or what they heard about these relatives. Some examples of books in this category include: *My Great-Aunt Arizona*, by Gloria Houston, *My Rotten, Redheaded Older Brother* by Patricia Polacco, *Mirandy and Brother Wind* by Patricia C. McKissack, and *Butterfly* by Patricia Polacco.

Next, I read aloud *Mirandy and Brother Wind* by Patricia McKissack.

In the author's note, McKissack explains that this story is based on her grandparents. She also explains the origins of the cakewalk. This book tells the story of a girl named Mirandy who wants to capture Brother Wind to be her partner for the junior cakewalk. She asks different people for advice on how to capture Brother Wind. Her clumsy friend, Ezel, appears in various scenes. She thinks he will take a different girl to the cakewalk. In the end, Mirandy asks Ezel to the cakewalk *and* she captures Brother Wind. Ezel and Mirandy dance with the wind, and they win first prize.

> **Mrs. G.:** I want to read you the author's note where she explains that the characters in this story are her grandparents. While I read the story, please listen for the elements we learned in characterization: character tags, strong voice, foreshadowing, feelings, white spaces, how characters change, contrast, and viewpoint.

After I read aloud the book, we had the following literary conversation:

> **Rivky:** The tag is Ezel is clutzy. It's foreshadowing, too, because Mirandy always knows that something is going to fall, or he's going to be clutzy and then he is.

> **Rachel:** It's also white spaces about the wind dancing with them. You have to imagine what that means and how he came to be dancing with them.

Aliza: You needed the Brother Wind in the story to make it good.

Mrs. G.: That's a great point. To create a memoir about a family story, the author adds the family members as characters and then she whips in imagination. I think imagination is a secret ingredient in memoir.

Kayla shares her horse-character story with kindergartners.

Interview a Family Member

Interview a family member about a family tale and write a story focusing on one main character. Include as many of the elements of characterization as you can, such as: contrast, character growth, foreshadowing, white spaces, a tag, and strong voice.

Final Thoughts

Through good literature, students analyze tools of characterization to use in their own writing. Children enjoy creating their own characters, and I find students' literary conversation rich when we focus on characterization. Students discover that story problems and conflicts grow from a character's fear, flaw, problem, or trait and that the solution to the story problem also lies within the traits of a story character. Studying character unlocks wonderful possibilities for young writers.

At recess one day recently, I heard two girls debating if Harry Potter is a flat or round character—*and what is his tag anyway?* I smiled and thought to myself, Hey, I *am* making a difference in these children's lives. Isn't that what teaching is all about?

Recommended Professional Books

Atwell, Nancy. *In the Middle*. Portsmouth, NH: Boynton-Cook Publications, 1998.

Avery, Carol. *And With a Light Touch*. Portsmouth, NH: Heinemann, 1993.

Bomer, Randy. *Time for Meaning*. Portsmouth, NH: Heinemann, 1995.

Calkins, Lucy McCormick. *The Art of Teaching Writing* (Second Edition). Portsmouth, NH: Heinemann, 1994.

Calkins, Lucy McCormick. *Living Between the Lines*. Portsmouth, NH: Heinemann, 1991

Edinger, Monica. *Using Beloved Classics to Deepen Comprehension*. New York: Scholastic Inc., 2001.

Egri, Lajos. *The Art of Dramatic Writing*. New York: Simon & Schuster, 1946, 1960.

Elwood, Maren. *Characters Make Your Story*. USA: The Writer Inc.   1942.

Fletcher, Ralph. *What a Writer Needs*. Portsmouth, NH: Heinemann, 1993.

Fletcher, Ralph and Portalupi, Joann. *Craft Lessons*. York, ME: Stenhouse Publishers, 1998

Fraser, Jane and Skolnick, Donna. *On Their Way*. Portsmouth, NH: Heinemann, 1994.

Hansen, Jane. *When Writers Read*. Portsmouth, NH: Heinemann, 1987.

Heard, Georgia. *For the Good of the Earth and Sun*. Portsmouth, NH: Heinemann, 1989.

Hindley, Joanne. *In the Company of Children*. York, ME: Stenhouse Publishers, 1996.

Kaplan, Michael, David. *Revision*. Cincinnati, OH: F&W Publications Inc., 1997.

Keene, Ellin, and Zimmermann, Susan. *Mosaic of Thought*. Portsmouth, NH: Heinemann, 1997.

Kurstedt, Rosanne and Koutras, Maria *Teaching Writing With Picture Books as Models* (Grades 4–8). New York: Scholastic Inc., 2000.

Mariconda, Barbara *The Most Wonderful Writing Lessons Ever* (Grades 2-4). New York: Scholastic Inc., 1999.

Routman, Regie *Invitations*. Portsmouth, NH: Heinemann, 1991.

Schaefer, Lola M. *Teaching Narrative Writing*. New York: Scholastic Inc., 2001.

Short, Kathy. *Literature As a Way of Knowing*. York, ME: Stenhouse Publishers, 1997.

Yopp, Hallie Kay and Yopp, Ruth *Literature-Based Reading Activities*. Nedham Heights, MA: Allyn & Bacon, 1992.

Recommended Books on Writing

Bauer, Marion Dane. *What's Your Story?* New York: Houghton Mifflin, 1992.

Brande, Dorothea. *Becoming a Writer*. New York: Harcourt Brace, 1934.

Brohaugh, William. *Write Tight*. Cincinnati, OH: Writer's Digest Books, 1993.

Conrad, Barnaby *The Complete Guide to Writing Fiction*. Cincinnati, OH: Writer's Digest Books, 1990.

Delton, Judy. *The 29 Most Common Writing Mistakes (And How to Avoid Them)*. Cincinnati, OH: Writer's Digest Books, 1985.

Dickson, Frank, and Smythe, Sandra. *The Writer's Digest Handbook of Short Story Writing*. Cincinnati, OH: Writer's Digest Books, 1970.

Elwood, Maren. *Characters Make Your Story*. Boston, MA: *The Write, Inc.*, 1942. (Reprinted by special arrangement with Houghton Mifflin. 1987).

Egri, Lajos. *The Art of Dramatic Writing*. New York: Simon & Schuster, 1946.

Fletcher, Ralph. *Live Writing*. New York: Avon Books, Inc., 1999.

——. *What a Writer Needs*. Portsmouth, NH: Heinemann, 1993.

——. *A Writers Notebook*. New York: Avon Camelot, 1996.

Gardner, John. *On Becoming a Novelist*. New York: HarperCollins, 1983.

Hall, Oakley. *The Art & Craft of Novel Writing*. Cincinnati, OH: Writer's Digest Books, 1989.

Kaplan, David, Michael. *Revision*. Cincinnati, OH: F7W Publications Inc, 1997.

Naylor, Reynolds, Phyllis. *How I Came To Be A Writer*. New York: Scholastic, Inc., 1987.

Ocork, Shannon. *How to Write Mysteries*. Cincinnati, OH: Writer's Digest Books, 1989.

Wyndham, Lee. *Writing For Children & Teenagers*. Cincinnati, OH: Writer's Digest Books, 1968.

Zinsser, William. *On Writing Well*. New York: HarperCollins, 1976.

Zinsser, Willam. *Inventing the Truth*. New York: Houghton Mifflin Company, 1998.

Suggested Books for Mini-Lessons on Characterization

Ahlberg, Janet and Allan. *The Jolly Postman*. Boston: Little, Brown, 1986.

Aliki. *The Two of Them*. New York: Morrow/Avon, 1987.

Allard, Harry and Marshall, James. *Miss Nelson Is Missing!* Boston: Houghton Mifflin Company, 1977.

Anholt, Laurence. *Degas and the Little Dancer*. London: Baron's, 1996.

Bemelmans, Ludwig. *Madeline*. New York: Puffin Books, 1977.

Blos, Joan W. *A Gathering of Days*. New York: Charles Scribner's Sons, 1979.

Blume, Judy. *The Pain and the Great One*. New York: Dell Books, 1974.

Brighton, Catherine. *The Picture*. Gordonsville, VA: Faber and Faber Limited, 1986.

Brinckloe, Julie. *Fireflies*. New York: Simon & Schuster, 1985.

Carlson, Nancy. *Harriet's Recital*. New York: Penguin Books, 1985.

——. *Loudmouth George and the Sixth-Grade Bully!* New York: Viking Penguin Inc, 1983.

Catling, Patrick Skene. *The Chocolate Touch*. New York: William Morrow & Co., 1952.

Cisneros, Sandra. "Eleven" *Woman Hollering Creek and Other Stories*. New York: Vintage Books, 1991.

——. *Hairs Pelitos*. New York: Alfred A. Knopf, 1994.

Cole, Joanna. *The Magic School Bus Lost in the Solar System*. New York: Scholastic Inc., 1990.

Condra, Estelle. *See the Ocean*. Nashville, TN: Ideals Children's Books, 1994.

Cooney, Barbara. *Roxaboxen*. New York: Penguin Books, 1991.

Curtis, Jamie Lee. *When I Was Little: A Four-Year-Old's Memoir of Her Youth*. New York: HarperCollins,1993.

Day, Alexandra. *Carl's Afternoon in the Park*. New York: Farrar, Straus & Giroux, 1991.

dePaola, Tomie. *The Art Lesson*. New York: G. P. Putnam & Sons, 1989.

Estes, Eleanor. *The Hundred Dresses*. New York: Harcourt, Brace, Jovanovich, 1944.

Freeman, Don. *Corduroy*. New York: Puffin Books, 1992.

Fox, Mem. *Harriet, You'll Drive Me Wild!* Florida: Harcourt Children's Books, 2000.

——. *Wilfrid Gordon McDonald Patrtridge*. New York: Kane/Miller Book Publishers, 1985.

Galbraith, Kathryn O. *Laura. Charlotte*. New York: Putnam & Grosset Group, 1990.

Gardner, John. *Stone Fox*. New York: HarperCollins, 1980.

Goodman, Joan Elizabeth. *Hope's Crossing*. New York: Scholastic Inc., 1998.

Greenfield, Eloise and Little, Lessie Jones. *Childtimes*. New York: HarperCollins, 1979.

Havill, Juanita. *Jamaica's Find*. Boston: Hougton Mifflin Company, 1986.

Heller, Ruth. *Many Luscious Lollipops: A Book About Adjectives*. New York: Penguin Putnam, 1989.

Hoban, Russell. *A Bargain for Frances*. New York: HarperCollins, 1970.

Houston, Gloria. *My Great-Aunt Arizona*. New York: HarperCollins, 1992.

Jeram, Anita. *Contrary Mary*. Cambridge, MA: Candlewick Press, 1995.

E. L. Konigsburg, *From the Mixed-Up Files of Mrs. Basil E. Frankweiler*. New York: Atheneum Books, 1970.

Lawson, Robert. *Ben and Me*. Boston, MA: Little Brown and Company, 1939.

Leaf, Munro. *The Story of Ferdinand*. New York: Penguin Book, 1936.

Little, Jean. *Hey World, Here I Am!* U.S.A.: HarperTrophy, 1986.

Lowry, Lois. *Number the Stars*. New York: Dell Publishing, 1989.

MacLachlan, Patricia. *Baby*. New York: Delacorte Press, 1993.

——. *Sarah, Plain and Tall*. New York: Scholastic, Inc., 1985.

MacDonald, Betty. *Mrs. Piggle-Wiggle's Magic*. New York: J. B. Lippincott Company, 1957.

Martin Jr., Bill and Archambault, John. *The Ghost-Eye Tree*. New York: Henry Holt, 1985.

McKissack, Patricia. *Mirandy and Brother Wind*. New York: Alfred A. Knopf, 1988.

Polacco, Patricia. *The Butterfly*. New York: Philomel Books, 2000.

——. *My Rotten, Redheaded Older Brother*. New York: Simon & Schuster, 1994.

——. *Thundercake*. New York: Penguin Putnam, 1990.

Rathmann, Peggy. *Ruby the Copycat*. New York: Scholastic, 1991.

Rylant, Cynthia. *Birthday Presents*. New York: Orchard Books, 1987.

———. *Night in the Country*. New York: Macmillan Publishing, 1991.

———. *The Relatives Came*. New York: Simon & Schuster, 1985.

Sendak, Maurice. *Pierre*. U.S.A.: HarperCollins, 1962.

Small, David. *Imogene's Antlers*. New York: Crown Publishers, 1985.

Sim, M. Dorrith. *In My Pocket*. Florida: Harcourt Brace & Company, 1996.

Steig, William. *Brave Irene*. Toronto: Collins Publishers, 1986.

Taylor, Mildred. *Roll of Thunder Hear My Cry*. New York: Penguin Putnam, 1976.

Viorst, Judith. *Alexander and the Terrible, Horrible, No Good, Very Bad Day*. New York: Atheneum Books, 1972.

———. *Earrings!* New York: Simon & Schuster, 1990.

Weiss, Nicki. *Princess Pearl*. New York: Puffin Books, 1987.

White, E. B. *Charlotte's Web*. New York: Bantam Books, 1986.

Wojciechowska, Maia. *Shadow of a Bull*. New York: Simon & Schuster, 1964.